# Three Ways
# To The One God

In the same series:

*The Lord's Prayer and Jewish Liturgy*
Edited by Jakob J. Petuchowski & Michael Brocke

*We Believe in One God*
Edited by Annemarie Schimmel & Abdoldjavad Falaturi

# Three Ways To The One God

## The Faith Experience in Judaism, Christianity and Islam

Edited by

Abdoldjavad Falaturi,
Jacob J. Petuchowski
and
Walter Strolz

Crossroad • New York

First published in USA 1987 by

The Crossroad Publishing Company
370 Lexington Avenue,
New York, NY 10022, USA.

First German version published as *Drei Wege zu dem einen Gott: Glaubenserfahrungen in den monotheistischen Religionen.*



Translated by John Griffiths, V. Green and J. Maxwell.



ISBN 0–8245–0818–1

Library of Congress Catalog Card No. 86–72308

Printed in Great Britain by
A Wheaton & Co Ltd. Exeter, England

Contents

# Foreword

The Oratio Dominica Foundation[1] had already held Jewish-Christian and Christian-Islamic colloquia (whose results have appeared in previous volumes in this series), when it was decided to invite representatives of the three great monotheistic religions to take part in further dialogue. This series of ecumenical colloquia is based upon a deep commitment to study of central aspects of faith in Judaism, Christianity and Islam. Naturally we cannot expect detailed treatments of specialized topics from so momentous an initial meeting of distinguished members of the three majors faiths. The contributions to the symposium on which this book is based explain and comment on fundamental standpoints of faith in divine revelation in time and history, and refer to their similarities and to their differences.

The persistent hope evident throughout this volume is the belief to which the Bible testifies: that God the Creator is also the Lord of history. The Koran, which does not acknowledge the notion of history as salvation history in the Judaeo-Christian sense,[2] says of God that He is the 'Lord of worlds' (Sura 1:2). According to the prophetic word of the Bible His loyalty (Is. 41 : 4; 54 : 5) comprises all that one whole glorious creation (cf. Koran 37 : 96, 22 : 76). It is irrevocable and therefore assures mankind from generation unto generation, but always anew, a possibility of life and a ground for hope. Jews and Christians also associate this faith-experience with the Fatherhood of God, which does not apply to Islam, though it has in common with Judaism and Christianity a faith in the one Creator God. In dialogue hitherto this faith has proved a common basis of trust. It proceeds in the light of the promise that, in spite of the somewhat profound contradictions between the monotheistic religions, the different professions of faith are not mutually exclusive but may be seen as comprised in God's transcendence. A shared belief in creation and faith in a Last Judgment are extended and indeed decisively marked by the historical experience that Jews, Christians and Muslims are children, or descendants, of Abraham (Gal. 3 : 29; Koran, Sura 22 : 78). That is the firm biblical ground of all believers in monotheism (Is. 51 : 1–2).

In his major commentary on Galatians,[3] Franz Mussner has interpreted the continuity of the promise made to Abraham and has shown what it means to say that in him all the nations of the earth are blessed. Nevertheless Abraham is also a somewhat contentious name, for Jews, Christians and Muslims make specific claims when appealing to their Abrahamic origin. It is a name which to date relies on no one principle of faith recognized by all three religions.

It is as important to remember this origin of faith in Abraham as to acknowledge freedom of confrontation, of dialogue, which must also include the possibility, and to some extent the necessity, of contradiction. One has to see the original 'thou' of a fellow human-being, of a partner in dialogue, behind all the words of Jewish, Christian and Muslim belief. We are too readily inclined to underestimate the ecumenical significance of this experience, which stems directly from the inalienable dignity of the human person. It shows that mankind points beyond the diversity of professions of faith and religions into the realm of ineffable mystery. That mysterious realm is the origin and support of all that believers can say to one another; before it they must all to some extent fall silent. Anyone who respects the mystery of the human person and, together with the Prophet, agrees that each individual is uniquely summoned by his own name, has access to the ontological essence and profundity of encounter between human beings. On that basis dialogue about faith, without any compulsion, is clearly an act of human freedom – and a free act of homage to God – the one God.

The main topics of this volume have been chosen and arranged to emphasize basic aspects of particular traditions of faith and the contemporary situation in each case. Both are necessary, for the human experience of faith takes place within this world and the dimension of time; it cannot move into a dimension outside history. All the contributions to this symposium rely essentially on faith in the uniqueness and incomparable nature of God – a faith which Jews, Christians and Muslims are coming increasingly to restore to its former importance as a source of historical and critical discernment. The prophetic element is given an equally strong emphasis. There are several signs that precisely this line of tradition could become most significant for continuing dialogue between Jews, Christians and Muslims. Some chapters of this book suggest that the biblical injunction not to make any graven image of God (2 Kings 20 : 1–4) is a hopeful signpost to a new era of human history. As monotheists consider the uniqueness of God, their recognition grows that the diverse ways to the one God are approximations to the mystery of God which unites and includes us all. In time, this kind of basic experience could produce a greater solidarity within the monotheistic religions, and a much more decisive understanding of their responsibility for the world. These considerations are of course subject to the promise that God, who summoned the generations from the beginning, is the Lord who is 'the first, and with the last' (Is. 41 : 4).

## Notes

[1] See Jakob J. Petuchowski & Michael Brocks, eds., The Lord' Prayer and Jewish Liturgy (London & New Rork, 1978); Annemarie Schimmel & Abdoldjavad Falaturi, eds., We Believe in One God (London & New York, 1979).

[2] Cf. A. Falaturi, 'Experience of Time and History in Islam', in: We Believe in One God, op. cit., pp. 63–76.

[3] F. Mussner, Der Galaterbrief (Freiburg im Breisgau, 1974).

# The Polarity of the Experience of God in the Prophecy of Israel

*Heinrich Gross*

It is inappropriate to talk about the prophecy of Israel in the usual Christian sense of prophecy, which is restricted to the biblical prophets. Instead our understanding of the Hebrew Bible should be based on a most significant aspect of revelation: that is, the persistence of prophecy during the entire period in which revelation was proclaimed in Israel. Hence all authentic mediators of revelation are prophets, for they are the figures commissioned to speak in a binding way, issuing both promises and precepts on God's behalf. This is, for instance, Martin Buber's acceptation of the prophecy of Israel in Sehertum: Anfang und Ende (Cologne & Olten, 1955) ('Abraham the Seer', in: Judaism, V. 4, 1956; 'Prophecy, Apocalyptic and the Historical Hour', in: Pointing the Way, London & New York, 1957).

## *1. The polarity of the experience of God in Israel and its contemporary environment*

To discover the right entry to our topic and to concentrate on essentials, it seems appropriate to compare Yahweh, the God of Israel, with the circumambient gods of Canaan, above all the most typical instance, the major deity Baal[1] , and to see Yahweh as antithetical to them.

The first major distinction in such a comparison is of course that Baal is a stationary god restricted to a certain location, whereas Yahweh is an accompanying God, the God of migration, a God who summons the people to be on their way. Baal is also named after the places at which he is especially revered: hence he is known as Baal Peor (Num. 23 : 28), as Baal Sebub (Sebul) (2 Kings 1 : 2–16), as Baal Zaphon (Ex. 14 : 2,9), as Baal Berith (Judg. 8 : 33), and in Baalbek as Baal of the Beka. Accordingly he would seem to be specially present in those places which are exceptionally fruitful. Clearly, the mythic mind which tends to personify the entire world – everything which is an object, 'it' – specially, and above all, personifies outstanding and sometimes quite lush vegetative forces. Primitive man, who is not yet in control of nature and the power of growth, and for whom they are not yet manipulable as they are for us, venerates this annually self-regenerative power which is the source of the growth and prosperity of plants, animals and human beings, and therefore of human life as a whole. He reveres it as a divine force, and ultimately projects it from his world, transferring it from below to above, and making it the chief deity in his pantheon. Since Baal appears every year at the same vital oases in the midst of the surrounding wilderness in the form of this vegetational force which is so decisive for life as a whole; since he appears as the life-bestowing god; and since he is a god who dies and rises again with the vegetation, he is experienced as a stationary, locational god who therefore has to be venerated religiously by analogy, and mainly in vegetative-sexual terms. On this basis the rite of the Sacred Wedding prevalent throughout the entire ancient Near East is wholly comprehensible. The Sacred Wedding, celebrated on New Year's Day by the King and Queen, by the High Priest and High Priestess, represents the fruits and fruitfulness of human, animal and vegetable life as the activity of Baal who is at work in vegetative power. Essentially he is nothing other than the personification of the vegetative force. Consequently the god Baal is entirely of this earth. He is the inward, driving and moving force in the individual areas of that which lives; the dynamic entelechy of life. Accordingly the god Baal himself is a part of the cosmos and subject to its fate which, in a consistent circuit, in the eternal return of that which is always the same, continuously repeats itself in accordance with the seasons.

The God of Israel, on the contrary, is the God who stands face to face with man, who relates Himself specially to man and comes towards him.[2] The first major experience which Israel was to have of its God in the time of the patriarchs and the early history of the nation, was that He enters the life of the elect from without, from above, breaking into the life of the patriarchs directly and without any human impulsion; that He is the accompanying God, the God who calls and provokes one to migrate and be on one's way in His company. Martin Buber is arguably right in suggesting that Israel in its early period experienced God not so much as the owner and proprietor of the land and of man, as is

Baal, but as the Leader, the Duke, and as its King.[3] Hence מֶלֶךְ as the name of God, and its derivation from מוֹלִיךְ as the term for God as King, and that of the participle hiphil from הָלַךְ. God therefore is the One who impels to movement, who makes one go; the One who precedes. Whatever the consequence of this ingenious interpretation of the predication of God as King, it certainly reveals the fundamental difference between the biblical, non-stationary God, who is not confined to a specific location, and the vegetation deities, Baal and Astarte, whose activity is reserved for places particular to each of them. The God Yahweh breaks into the life of Israel from without and from above. He makes a direct incursion into his people. The patriarchs experience Him in precise counter-movement to their perception of the god Baal, for the fertility god emerges from within nature and then, as befits a deity, is projected into heaven. If Baal is the personification and projection of the force of vegetation from below to above, the deified manifestation of the mysterious inward life-force, Yahweh for His part, spontaneously and of His own initiative, impelled by nothing earthly or human, breaks from above into the life of the first-chosen Abraham and Israel. He confers Himself directly on His people and is therefore necessarily, in contrast to Baal, essentially non-discernible in the created world; therefore He is also inconceivable and underivable for the human mind. The Bible calls this special actualization of God His epiphany, the appearance or manifestation of God, though ultimately still in a veiled form, and always to selected individuals or to the whole people. God's appearance as a basis for the process of revelation is therefore always dialogical in form. It occurs and is fulfilled in His word expressed to the elect; it offers instruction and awaits the answer of man who is summoned to make a free decision for God. Every epiphany is a triad: God appears (literally: He allows Himself to be seen); God speaks; God makes a promise and requires something. This triad is maintained in all manifestations of God in the Old Testament, whether in the case of Abraham (Gen. 12 : 18; 22), of Moses and the chosen people (Ex. 3 : 19; 20), of Elijah (1 Kings 19), or even of the major prophets: Isaiah (Is. 6), Jeremiah (Jer. 1) and Ezekiel (Ez. 1–3).

Furthermore this God is obviously distinguished and raised above Baal by His oneness and uniqueness, which He jealously defends. The Decalogue maintains that for Israel there can be no other God than this God as firmly as it forbids adultery and murder (Ex. 20 : 3; Deut. 5 : 7). Moreover the fact that Yahweh has no divine consort, and indeed the fact that every care is taken to avoid even the slightest indication that this might be so, and that the Bible speaks with such restraint and marked reserve in this regard (cf., for instance, the song of the love of God in Hos. 11), indicates a conscious disavowal in the Old Testament of the concepts of God prevalent in the circumambient world in which the force of vegetation, and consequently the divine couple, were pre-eminently significant. The uniqueness of this biblical stance is shown by the Jewish colony in Elephantine in Upper Egypt where, after early separation from the prophetic injunctions of the mother country, and under the pressure of Egyptian religion, which was multiform and difficult to understand, the God Yahweh was given a divine spouse.

The fact that Yahweh does not exist as the hidden centre, and therefore does not emerge from mundane things as their proper inner essence to become perceptible like Baal, but actually exists beyond them and surpasses them all, is also patent in the background of the second commandment of the Decalogue, according to which to make an image of God is a capital offence (Ex. 20 : 4-6; Deut. 5 : 8–10). This interdiction, which forbids any attempt to portray God by a human yardstick and to understand him according to human standards, and therefore contains a merciless verdict on the religious notions of the milieu surrounding Israel, was deeply embedded in the faith of the nation. This is confirmed by the scorn and irony which are directed against the makers of divine images in Is. 44 : 9–20 and Jer. 10 : 1–16. Here it is a question of the complete immanence of God as against His transcendence, His complete insertion into the human world and therefore His complete humanization – which is necessarily an abrogation of His divinity, as against the wholly different structure but human way in which He breaks out of His reserved transcendent world in revelation and redemptive action, to enter in a quite emphatically anthropomorphic mode into human life.

One final instance may serve to indicate and characterize this distinction between Yahweh and Baal. The fact that Baal is immanent and inherent in the course of earthly things, growth and prosperity, and is indeed their very motive centre, is shown by the way in which he is woven into the course of things, the return of the same, the year's cycle, and the repeated death and resurrection of nature. Consequently we have the cult of Baal which by analogous procedures and rites tried to influence this periodical round favourably. In this perspective it is hardly coincidental that in Israel Yahweh was not experienced initially as the Creator God, and therefore primarily as the God of nature, but that Yahweh from the start, so to speak, entered without any mediation, ex abrupto, into the historical life of the patriarchs and henceforth co-determined the course and goal of this historical life as its protagonist. That meant an exit from the eternally recurrent cycle of the return of the same as prescribed and made possible for man by God. Yahweh thereby placed Himself outside and above all fateful events, showed that He was superior to them, and by His action in salvation history simultaneously withdrewsthe life of His elect from them. From Abraham onwards, God's field of activity is essentially the special area of human existence. His efforts are aimed much more directly at the lives of men in their historical existence than at man in creation, at human involvement in nature and association with nature.

Man in his createdness is the substrate for the historical existence which he has to realize. Inasmuch as God codetermines and co-effects human history in a special way, it becomes salvation history. It is that form of history uniquely singled out so that the salvation which God offers mankind is imparted to us from it and in it. Accordingly the man–God relationship has a basic structure quite different from that of the religion of Baal. This is obvious in the form of worship of the religion of revelation, which is essentially memoria, a cult of reminiscence. Worship in revealed religion is not primarily concerned with the thriving growth of vegetation, whether human, animal or plant, desired and petitioned for by means of rites and rituals analogous to the force of vegetation. It is much more a matter of the continuing actuality of the great actions of God in the history of Israel, by means of which believers have continual access to divine salvation. The specific characteristic of worship in revealed religion is that by virtue of it the salvific action of God in history, and its supratemporal salvific efficacy, can co-exist with every period of time, and that the commemorative cult is the location provided by God where in every age this salvation is actually applied to the believer. This is shown by the Passover, the most important feast, which is celebrated anew every year as a memorial enactment of God's great action of redemption and liberation in the exodus from Egypt (Ex. 12:14, 24–8), and by the Jewish understanding of this prescription (Pesach–Haggadah X, b5), where we read: 'In every age everyone is bound to look upon himself as if he himself had made the exodus from Egypt. Therefore we are bound to thank, to revere the One who did all these miracles to us and to our fathers. He led us out of slavery into freedom...'

I cannot find a better way of concluding this confrontation of Yahweh and Baal than by quoting Martin Buber: 'Every nation elevates itself as an absolute and adores it as such. Israel experiences the Absolute as that which Israel itself is not and which it cannot itself become, and honours it as such. Or, furthermore: The nations can experience the absolute only in what they are. For Israel the Absolute can be experienced only if and because it confronts that which we are. And, furthermore: To be enclosed in self means to be condemned to die; to exist in orientation towards the Illimitable means to be redeemed from death. The deification of the nation and the death of the nation are closely connected'.[4] This quotation is a philosophically profound and exact summary of the foregoing biblical differences and contradictions between Baal and Yahweh. It is the opposition which is reflected in the undeviating struggle of the prodigious Elijah, and is eloquently expressed in the book of Hosea.

## *2. The polarity of the experience of God in the Old Testament*

The biblical polarity of Israel's experience of God can be presented appropriately and meaningfully only against this perhaps somewhat broadly sketched background. In addition one might perhaps cite as a result of the foregoing the fact that what is essential and specific to the biblical God consists in his transcendence, which is so far removed from the world and from mankind; as if God dwelled far removed from man and from the earth in His preordained world and only made occasional incursions into human destiny, but in general left things to proceed on their own, like a piece of clockwork which He had left to unwind. Anyone inclined to see the biblical God thus will soon receive another image of Him on closer acquaintance with the Old Testament. For the God Yahweh cannot be properly experienced and understood, in so far as that is possible at all for men, only by considering His supra-mundane essence, His sublimity and transcendence. Rather, perhaps even greater attention must be given to the other pole: his entry into the world, into the life of mankind. As Gerhard von Rad says, we have to look directly at His 'penetrative will to immanence', because it is there that God allows Himself to be seen and reveals Himself as He really is, and because consequently it is there that knowledge of God becomes possible.

The fact that the Bible as a whole largely articulated its statements most effectively in terms of oppositions also depends on the nature of Hebrew grammar. For instance, 'large and small' is used to express the whole nation, and 'from Dan to Beersheba' the entire Promised Land. Grammar also certainly represents the fundamental and most characteristic expression of a nation's mode of thought. The two revealed names of the Old Testament God, 'Yahweh' and 'the Holy One of Israel', are striking proof that this dualistic form of expression is also most appropriate to any representation of and approximation to the God of revelation. El is the general Semitic designation for God. After the Patriarchs had unhesitatingly adopted it, and in its manifold biblical form an appropriate term was also available for God as conceived in revealed religion (by derivation and significance, El is an expression of the might of the One named thus Who transcends mankind and the universe), Moses asked the God of the Patriarchs to reveal His name. The name Yahweh revealed to Moses, however it is interpreted, is essentially non-qualitative and describes nothing of the Nature of God (as long as one forsakes the conceptual and terminological practice of dogmatic theology in combining God's essence with His activity). Instead the name Yahweh continues the term El as used of God; and specifically, inasmuch as the name Yahweh indicates that the whole might of God expressed in El, in Elohim, is present to and for Israel and is applied to Israel. Hence in the name Yahweh God is referred to most strikingly in terms of his lasting commitment to his people and for his people; to such an extent that even God's nature can be described in terms of this commitment to the chosen people. Therefore Yahweh is to be described as the God who always emerges anew from His transcendence to enter into human life, takes human history into His hands, and steers the course of human life towards salvation.

The title 'the Holy One of Israel', on the other hand, initially indicated the supramundane sublimity of God, His separation from any creature: as the God who exists in absolute completion and perfection in the world preordained for Him alone, to such an extent indeed that even the highest orders of angels are sealed, as it were, by His glory (cf. Is. 6 : 1–3). And yet His holiness does not indicate a stationary, absolutely self-contained mode of divine existence, but is also ruled by a penetrative power which appears in the all-piercing rays of God's glory. Both creation and the course of salvation are penetrated by this divine holiness which pours out into the universe; they are permeated by this divine self-glorification which determines all world history and all salvation history. Hence the salvific process which God bestows upon man is essentially the reverse side of the process of God's glorification, which affects all world history and, in spite of this constant penetration, of itself apprehends and forms all things without any chance of exhaustion. In spite of all the penetrative power and ability of God's holiness as glory, as God's revealed holiness this glory exceeds all earthly and human measures, and, in spite of all God's concern for man, places him in a position of obedient distance from God. Man can approach this glorious God and the divine glory only in humble homage. An instance of this is Moses on Mount Sinai before the glory of God (Ex. 24 : 15–8), which in a spiritualized form supersedes the presence of God on the Ark of the Covenant in the post-exilic period (cf. Ex. 33 : 18–23; Is. 6 : 3–7).

This ultimate commitment to His people (which is derived from His nature) and hence His entry into the destiny of His elect are responsible for the fact that, on the one hand, God is portrayed in an emphatically anthropomorphic fashion throughout the entire Old Testament: God sees and hears; He speaks and even cries out. God experiences feelings of love, pity and mercy; He exhibits anger and is vengeful; He shows remorse and changes His mind; He even roars like a lion (Am. 3 : 8). On the other hand, the Decalogue is just as unambiguous and absolute in its injunction against making an image of this anthropomorphically conceived God as in forbidding adultery and murder (Ex. 20 : 4–6; Deut. 5 : 8–10). To make an image of God means trying to reduce God to human measure, and to secure something of and in Him in a human representation. It means establishing a cult at whose centre there is ultimately a God made by man, and therefore one subject to man; which in the end would mean forcing Yahweh into the cast of Baal and baalizing Him. God must withdraw from any such endeavour, for it would signify that His illimitability was limited, and deprive Him of His infinity which exceeds all that is human and worldly. Finally, God has made an image of Himself. The crown of human existence is that every man and woman is the image and likeness of God and therefore a bearer of His majesty on the face of the earth.[5] But if God Himself places His image on earth in the shape of man, then, according to the Old Testament and contemporary notions of image-making, it is wholly inappropriate for man to manufacture an image of God.

The fact that, in spite of all the distance between God and the world and mankind, the Bible is so intent on representing God in human form is also the basis of God's ability and readiness to enter into dialogue with man. By making man in His image and likeness, God has made man capable of dialogue with Him. Perhaps the most profound meaning of creation is to be found in the fact that God allows it to culminate in man, as His counterpart capable of dialogue with Him, and His authentic partner. Hence it is not surprising that revelation characteristically takes the form of dialogue; the word of God is addressed to man, and requires an answer from man.

God's commitment to Israel, which is assured for ever in His name, is so far-reaching that Yahweh takes up His residence among His people. The God of Sion emerges from the migration deity of the migrant people of God in the primitive period of its history in the Promised Land, from the God of Sinai, and in exodus from Egypt. Numerous Old Testament texts testify to this. The Psalms above all transfer all the prerogatives of Sinai (Ps. 68) to Sion.[6] On the mercy seat of the Ark of the Covenant, on the gold plate, Yahweh is invisibly present in an especially emphatic way. It is a mode of presence which extends far beyond His ubiquitousness in the entire creation, with which the Old Testament is well acquainted.[7] Yet in spite of the intensity of His presence in the Temple, and in spite of the local delimitation of His special presence on the mercy-seat of the Ark, here too Yahweh remains invisible; He is not so to speak assumed into and enclosed in created existence, as happens in the cult of the Golden Calf (Ex. 32), and the bull shrines in Bethel and Dan in the case of the deities adored there and conceived similarly to Baal

(1 Kings 12 : 26–33). This cult manifests the continual danger that Israel would baalize Yahweh and conceive Him in the manner of the vegetation god. Here the boundary between the transcendent-immanent God and immanence is transgressed right up to the point of the full abrogation of His transcendence, so that God is de facto deprived of His divinity and humanized. But the humanization of God and the incarnation of God are two fundamentally different things. Rather Yahweh, in spite of His special presence in the Temple, henceforth transcends the entire objective world. He is elevated, as the dream of summons of Isaiah (Is. 6) sees it, to cosmic dimensions; and, according to Ez. 1–3, rises above all cosmic ties and bounds, and dwells properly speaking in His heavenly world, which transcends all that is created – as a whole series of Old Testament texts declare.[8]

Yahweh, who is simultaneously God near and distant, is also and above all present in Israel in His word. It is the unique prerogative of the Chosen People, that God should be so close to it (cf. Deut. 7), and yet can never become wholly comprehensible and conceivable in His word, but remains inconceivable. Every revelation of God (which is ultimately always mysterious) reveals the profound reason for Job's dilemma, for God shows himself to Job in a quite unknown aspect; the problem is that he can no longer understand the God who was so closely associated with him in good times. Neither God nor His name, neither His glory nor anything of Him is ever revealed so very clearly to mankind as to be perceptible to the very core. These things are veiled and hidden in the light-and-darkness of the divine mystery. Every revelation necessarily affords a greater degree of mystery, a greater plus of mysterious divine darkness than man could ever comprehend. It is never possible for man, even when closest to God, to get to the bottom of God (Ps. 44; 77). In spite of His dual presence (for example, during the exodus from Egypt in the angel of Yahweh, in the cloud and pillar of fire), God remains as hidden as Yahweh who encloses Himself in the thunder and lightning and thick cloud on Sinai, and in the Decalogue gives His People the Magna Charta of the Sinaitic Covenant (Ex. 19–20).

Moreoever, as revelation grows, the distance between God and man increases. When God appears to Abraham in the form of three men (Gen. 18 f), in the form of Yahweh Mal'ak, in unusual proximity and almost as intimately as a close friend (Yahweh Mal'ak is a form of appearance which remains effective through

Moses up to Joshua; Ex. 3; Jos. 5 : 13–5), later on, from one stage to the next, we notice an increasing distance between God and mankind: whether it is a question of an increasing displacement towards the invisible, unveiling-veiling word, or one of an emergence of God into cosmic spaces and dimensions – even spaces and dimensions which surpass the cosmos.[9] Parallel to this there is an increasing distance between man and God and an increasing human awe before God. The angels, as God's messengers, bridge this gulf. This development is taken so far that in the late Old Testament period no one any longer dares even pronounce the name of God.[10] Right into the New Testament veiled language is used for God: 'heaven', for instance, or 'the angels'.

Whether the course of biblical narrative at times moves quite close to the known God, as with Abraham and Moses, or God withdraws into an almost ineffable and incomprehensible distance, as in the later prophets (Zech., Dan.), when an interpreting angel is required to understand visions, nowhere in the Old Testament is the polarity in the various forms and possibilities of the experience of and encounter with God that I have described entirely surrendered in favour of one or other aspect. This fact derives not only from the absolute supramundane nature of God, but is also grounded in the process (which involves all world history) of His glorification in the entire cosmos, and above all in man, for whom this glorification of God ultimately means God's salvific action working upon him and God's salvation in him. In this opposition, God is most profoundly experienced as the Living One per se who marvellously controls the course of things, and in so doing above all respects human freedom and directs His action accordingly. He is often the subject of Joseph's words to his brothers in Gen. 50 : 20: 'As for you, you meant evil against me; but God meant it (חָשַׁב) for good'. The varying conception of God noticeable all along the course of revelation, together with His purposeful interference in human activity and His redirection of it, are unique indications of the vitality of the biblical God, who emerges ever anew from His transcendence and enters into human life and striving, in order to direct human attention to the actual transcendental nature of God and to form man accordingly.

I must mention yet another aspect of God's approach to man. Yahweh approaches His people not only in an anthropomorphic form, but enters into the existence of some of the elect so very far beyond the imparting of His word that they, in so far as that is possible, represent God in their lives and therefore live 'theomorphically'. This is particularly striking in the lives of the prophets Hosea and Jeremiah.[11] In them revelation not only descends as a still incomprehensible divine word to the borders of human discourse, but in addition Yahweh through the mouth of a messenger lays claim to the prophet's whole life, without reservation, for the announcement of his requirements and promise. At God's behest, Hosea marries a temple prostitute (an initiate, according to H.W. Wolff[12]), in order thus to represent typologically the entire intimate association of Yahweh with the Chosen People (Hos. 1–3). Just as the prophet's wife becomes unfaithful, and Hosea himself profoundly experiences God's deep pain and is forced even to punish his wife, so God out of harsh necessity withdraws from Israel the gifts of the Covenant: grace, mercy and election. It is hardly possible to find a more penetrating and lasting form of proclamation than in the prophet's life, which is wholly claimed by God, and to conceive of a greater closeness than that of God to Hosea, which verges on complete divine identification. Here we have a unique expression of the imitation of God as the prophet's duty laid upon him by God. In his life and his way of life he has to represent God exclusively, and wholly to negate his own aims and wishes.

The situation is quite different with Jeremiah, who has to bear the burden of God as no other prophet. God drags this sensitive man, who prefers the quiet, withdrawn and solitary life proper to his nature, into the harsh light of a public world opposed to God. He forces Jeremiah so severely into the totality of His service as to demand celibacy from him and thereby force him to surrender every aspect of his private life. This total commitment to proclamation which God demands, and God's intended total representation of the divine approach to Israel in the prophet's life and service, lead to the profound spiritual conflict so poignantly expressed in the Confessiones Jeremiae.[13] Here an unwonted closeness of God is present in the life and destiny of the elect, which then however shifts from God to the far-distant God in that profound conflict and apparently total divine abandonment and surrender of the prophet. Here we have a foretaste of what the mystics were later to call the dark night of the soul.

The passionately vital and at the same time dual and inconceivably tense existence and action of Yahweh can be seen in an especially impressive form in Hos. 11, the Old Testament hymn to the love of God.[14] Verses 8 f above all are the centre and goal of this summation of revelation and salvation history; they are indeed the prototype of all histories of theology:

> How can I give you up, O Ephraim!
> How can I hand you over, O Israel!
> How can I make you like Admah!
> How can I treat you like Zeboiim.
> My heart recoils within me,
> My compassion grows warm and tender.
> I will not execute my fierce anger,
> I will not again destroy Ephraim;
> For I am God and not man,
> The Holy One in your midst,
> And I will not come and destroy.

The context of Hos. 11 demands of God that he should proceed according to the measure of his justice; that destiny should take its course; and that Israel should undergo destructive judgment. Yet the unexpected and unheard-of thing happens. To enable one to grasp this incomprehensible about-turn, the prophet offers an insight into the deepest level of the divine nature: he appeals from God to God, from God's justice to God's heart as the last court of judgment for God's behaviour. It is contrary to God's heart to carry out his own just sentence on Israel, to allow Israel to fall back from its elect position to the level of the many surrounding nations. The verb הפך which Genesis 19 : 25 uses to describe the total destruction of Sodom and Gomorrah, is used in Hos. 11 : 8 for the entry of love into the heart of God in favour of His people. God contradicts Himself, as it were, says No to Himself and to His justice, so that of His mercy He can still say Yes to His people, against all rational understanding and beyond all human calculation. God upsets the layers of His own heart in order once again to be able to bestow His love on His people, to an inconceivable extent, and one that is no longer rationally comprehensible. The transgressions of Israel and the reaction of divine anger move Yahweh to exceed His own possibilities and afford new space for the creative power of His incomparable love, to allow it a hitherto unknown dimension of operation, and thus to demonstrate a new and infinitely profound aspect of the dynamic power of God's love for his people. Merciful love wins a victory over God's inalienable justice. The ground of this unexpected change of divine attitude, for God's compassion, is unusual: God is the Holy One. The nature and person of this God who is the Holy One are therefore profoundly determined by love. Hence not divine power, which is ruled by justice, and not holiness, in the face of which all that is imperfect is consumed (cf. Is. 6 : 5), are the ultimate determining factors of divine nature and action, but the love of God. Power and holiness in God are therefore oriented to the centre of His love; are controlled and ruled by it; and where necessary (as in Hos. 11) are even, as far as their dispositions are concerned, turned upside down and re-oriented. To put it paradoxically, God inclines to man more than to Himself. In the interests of His people, God says No to Himself, and draws on ever more profound levels of His love, in order to be able to say a boundless Yes to His people. As the deepest expression of His nature, the love of God is that aspect of Him in which all discordant and accordant details of revelation come together, and in which the polarity of the prophet's experience of God is sublated into a higher, spreading unity. God's love is the unifying factor of even the seemingly quite disparate statements made by God. His love is creative power, the ultimate pronouncement about God; in it the vitality of God shines, blossoms and is fruitful. In it every form of experience of God is composed in a way inconceivable in earthly terms. In it, therefore, man reaches, by way of knowledge of God and beyond it (by way of a knowledge of God understood, that is, biblically in the sense of Hosea and Ezekiel), an ultimate and most intimate association with God which is the most profound form of love: one which shows ever and again that it is love alive and love abounding. In this ineffable love of God all the dualism of the experience of God in history and in creation, in revelation and in salvation, is brought together and raised up as the unifying centre, and recognized as the creative and redemptive divine vitality.

## Notes

1 See H. Vorländer, Mein Gott. Die Vorstellungen vom persönlichen Gott im Alten Orient und im Alten Testament (Kevelaer-Neukirchen, 1975). On Baal see J. Kühlewein, article on ba'al in ThHWAT, I (Munich, 1971), pp. 327–33, and De Moor & Mulder, article on ba'al in ThWAT, I (Stuttgart, 1972), pp. 706–27.

2 See Cross, article on 'el in ThWAT, I (Stuttgart, 1971), pp. 259–70 and W.H.Schmidt, article on 'el in ThHWAT, I (Munich, 1971), pp. 142–9.

3 Cf. M. Buber, Königtum Gottes (Werke, Vol. II) (Munich, 1964), pp. 489–723 (ET: The Kingship of God, New York, 1966).

4 M. Buber, Die Götter der Völker und Gott (Werke, Vol. II) (Munich, 1964), pp. 1069–83, 1069 (ET: 'The Gods of the Nation and God', in: Israel and the world (New York, 1948).

5 Cf. Gen. 1 : 26–8; Ps. 145 : 12.

6 Cf., e.g., Ps. 15; 24; 48; 50; 84; 122; 132, but also 2 Sam. 6; 1 Kings 8.

7 Cf. Ps. 139 : 7–12; Job 23 : 8–10; Jonah.

8 Dan. 7 : 10–4; Ps. 113; 115 : 16.

9 As is clear from a comparison of Is. 6; Jer. 1; Ez. 1–3; Dan. 7 : 10–4.

10 See the Septuagint translation of Lev. 24 : 16; the mere citation of the divine name arose from the original misuse of the name of God.

11 Cf. in this regard U. Mauer, Gottesbild und Menschwerdung (Tübingen, 1971), especially pp. 46–114.

12 See H.W. Wolff, Dodekapropheton 1: Hosea (Neukirchen, second edition, 1965), pp. 1–26.

13 Jer. 15 : 10–21; 16 : 1–9; 20 : 7–18.

14 Cf. in this regard H. Gross, 'Das Hohelied der Liebe Gottes', in 'Zur Theologie von Hosea 11', in: Mysterium der Gnade (Regensburg, 1975), pp. 83–91.

# Timelessness and the Historical Reality of the Torah

*Albert H. Friedlander*

## I.

In 1964 Martin Buber sent the following message to a gathering which in a certain sense was very similar to the colloquium on which this book is based: 'There can be no question of the religions of the world reaching agreement about their articles of faith. That is neither appropriate to them, nor would they succeed in any such attempt: it is a matter for God alone. It can only be a matter of the religions of the world discussing and confronting human salvation together before the point of collapse. That, after all, is their task'.[1]

Ernst Simon, to whom this message was entrusted, also spoke of the experience of faith: not of the 'wholly Other' who joins us all together (that is, of God), but of the 'shattered Other' – God's manifestation in the affirmative religions. He asked these questions: How can each of us on the basis of his own belief learn to understand better the standpoint of another, even if he cannot reach agreement with that other person in matters dogmatic? And: What can each of us do to ensure that our believing existence reinforces the humanity of our non-believing neighbours (that is, those who are not adherents of any religions), and thus contributes to the salvation of mankind? Jews, Christians and Muslims can enter into dialogue on the basis of these questions and fight side-by-side against disaster. Each of us is a witness; each of us learns and teaches. Yet all of us say too little. Faith and the experience of faith are partly handed on in words which mean something different in each tradition, in an age of which Karl Wolfskehl said:

> And though you have a thousand words,
> The word, the word is dead.

Experience moreover is faith and doubt, the God who is close and the God who is distant. None of us can speak about the Jewish experience of faith without mentioning the polarities which are evident in revelation and in testimony. And can we really feel so removed from our so-called 'religiously unbelieving neighbour'? The Jewish faith-experience of the twentieth century is better acquainted with night than with day, and the testimony of the non-believing experience of the distant God has to be included in our dialogue. The imagery of Paul Celan is directly relevant here:

In the almond – what dwells in the almond?
Nothing.
What dwells in the almond is Nothing.
There it dwells and dwells.

In Nothing – what dwells there? The King.
There the King dwells, the King.
There he dwells and dwells.

Jew's curl, you'll not turn grey.

And your eye – on what does your eye dwell?
On the almond your eye dwells.
Your eye, on Nothing it dwells.
Dwells on the King, to him remains loyal, true.
So it dwells and dwells.

Human curl, you'll not turn grey.
Empty almond, royal-blue.[2]

The bitter almond of Jewish life contains human and divine suffering. The faith-experiences of the King's people comprise the covenant of the Torah, within and without history. The question of the 'timelessness and historical reality of the Torah' is posed from without. There are answers in Jewish scholarship, in biblical exegesis, in philosophy and in theology. The Torah is a timeless revelation which takes effect in history. That is also an article of Christian and Muslim faith. But are we contributing to this colloquium in order to confirm this faith mutually? That is a matter for God alone (and our personal experience of faith). The only answers which we can try to give are the answers of Jewish life at the moment. Open the almond. Break it open:

In the almond – what dwells in the almond?
Nothing.
...
In Nothing – what dwells there? The King.

In 63 BC Pompey was the first non-Jew to enter the Temple. At first the priests continued their work as if nothing had happened. Some were killed by the soldiers. Pompey stopped the killing and entered the Holy of Holies. What did he see there? Nothing. For him the shrine of the Jews was empty. Even now, two thousand years later, the request is made from without that a regular and well-ordered Judaism should expound its dogmas and testimonies to revelation to a group of experts. The important aspect of these colloquia is their avoidance of that particular tendency. What takes place is dialogue; and we hear not one but all the voices of Judaism. Elie Wiesel spoke of the God who hung from the gallows in Auschwitz. Paul Celan told us of the Nothing in the almond. Jakov Lind sings his Heine ballad of the knight without chattels and all, all are the crackling tongues of the flame which bursts forth from the burning bush. Sinai burns. And the Temple. And those recent years. And the Torah: black flames on white flames, timeless words within Jewish existence. Do not ask me whether a world without Jews is a world without the Torah. But a world without the Torah is a world without Jews.

## II

There are still Jews; and they are all members of the shalshelet ha-quabbalah, the golden chain of mediation, of interpretation, of the torah she-be'al peh, of the Oral Torah, or Oral Law, which has been handed down from Sinai to our own times. Not every word has the same authority, and there are wrong roads which lead into the sands of the wilderness. But the timelessness of the Torah covenant brings them all together, and we know that Israel wrestles with itself in the dark nights in order to find the way to truth. In the light of dawn we limp away from the place of struggle in order to bear witness anew to the covenant. It is never a dogma, but always an experience. Jakob Petuchowski and I had the same teacher whose words are also discernible in Jakob's article – Leo Baeck. In the dark night of Theresienstadt Leo Baeck wrote of the covenant of the One: 'That this One lives, is eternal and rules everywhere has become the faith of this people. It has constantly been confirmed in that certainty. Everything proceeds from and towards the One. There is a Law which the one God has instituted. He has established it in the world and in mankind. There is the covenant, the covenant of the one God with the universe and with the nations of the earth: there is nothing outside the Law and nothing without it. And it exists, the special certainty within this inclusive certainty, the Law of this people, of this people which was summoned by the one God to the Law, so that the Law of God should become its life and its future – this covenant of God with it and its history within the covenant with the world and what resides in it'.[3]

When the prophets describe the polarity of the experience of God, they express an inward experience of Israel, an experience in this One, with this One, together with Him and yet over against Him, so to speak always encircled by Him and seen and heard by Him... always espoused and acknowledged and held fast (Baeck). The covenant is not only for the elect; mankind lives in it. Samson falls throughout the centuries. One generation perishes and another rises up. But the earth remains for ever. And the synagogues stand in every age, and the rhythmic reading of the Torah fills the space and offers the laws of revelation, which become commandments in decisive times. There are three accounts in the first book of covenants in which God is one of the partners: the first covenant, with the generations of man, between Noah and God, secures the world and time. The second, between God and Abraham, promises him the Holy Land; the third, between God and Abraham, bestows with circumcision the timeless covenant between God and the descendants of Abraham. Concentric, narrowing circles[4] testify that the world, mankind and Israel have become God's partners. Partnership presupposes reciprocality, even if one partner is incomparably superior. Israel finds conditions for living and a direction for life in the Torah covenant, fundamental conditions for life between Israel and God, and Israel and the nations. The most characteristic aspect of Israel, the Sabbath, confirms the relationship with the world and with mankind, because it keeps the covenant between Israel and God at the midpoint of Jewish life. Baeck writes of the words of the covenant: 'The law of rhythm is included in it, by which week after week creation and institution become one in the soul of this people, the law of the Sabbath: ... a sign for ever'.

But it is not only an everlasting sign. The b$^{e}$rith of the Torah, the covenant, the shabbat of the Torah, this sacred rhythm – here realities of Jewish life today are apparent. Sabbath is not only doctrine, illuminated by the dream of the messianic Kingdom at the end of days. Shabbat and b$^{e}$rith are divine questions which are answered in Jewish life. The tragic aspect of Jewish existence is that the answer is never complete: one is always on the way – the timeless, unending way –, the individual and the group cannot reach the goal. The rabbis said that at the moment when a Sabbath was fully celebrated the messianic age would begin for the world.

The tragic notion that man always falls by his own fault is alive in the Torah. Jacob or Moses, Rebekah or Miriam – for revelation appears through the life of the generations, and the history of the ancestors has as much to say to us as the laws in Leviticus. George Steiner in The Death of Tragedy will not allow that the Jewish attitude to the world is properly tragic. He argues that damages and compensation may be classed as justice but not as tragedy, and that the demand for justice is both the pride and the burden of the Jewish tradition. In the end there is no doubt that God's behaviour to man is just and even rational, even though his intervention often seems unbearably slow. Steiner remarks that the Old Testament sees catastrophe as a specific moral lack or inadequate comprehension, whereas the Greek tragedians saw the forces shaping and destroying our lives as lying outside the rule of reason and justice; for the Jews there was a miraculous continuity between knowledge and action, whereas for the Greeks a gulf of irony lay between them.[5]

If we look at the teachings of the Torah, we discover that Steiner is right:

> This commandment that I give you today
> is not withdrawn from you, not distant.
> It is not in heaven that you spoke:
> Who goes up to heaven and brings it to us
> and gives it to us so that we may hear it and do it?...
> No, the word is very close to you,
> in your mouth and in your heart,
> that it may be done.
>
> (Deut. 30 : 12 ff; from the Buber-Rosenzweig translation.)

The Torah sees the connection between knowing and doing. Eternal justice prevails in the world. But if we put life in the Torah alongside teaching, we also perceive the dimensions of tragedy and irony in the text. The covenant between man and God brings eternal justice, even if the reward is bestowed only upon other times and other men: Sabbath is a word of hope for all men, a small fragment of the future, to lead people in the paths of righteousness. But the tragedies of individual life still exist. On the next day, on the Sabbath, we read in the Synagogue how the blind Isaac blesses the younger son Jacob. We hear of the wild anger and fury of Esau and watch Rebekah who settles everything. And all that is woven together in the teachings, a revelation of the divine plan in which everything is in the end as it should be. But in the lives of the protagonists we see only suffering and pain. Rebekah sends her beloved son far away for a short time. For twenty years he will work for others and she will never see him again. Jacob himself follows a hard road that leads to greatness. In the end he can only say to Pharaoh: 'Few and evil have been the days of the years of my life' (Gen. 47). And even if we say that all that passes in the light of eternal justice, we find an element of tragedy in the Torah: for man lives in the Torah, and life has its tragic dimension. Jewish history is toldot and not historia. The chain of the generations brings living words into time and into the world, and the Torah offers us doctrine and life.

Israel encounters the timelessness and historical effectiveness of the Torah in every age. The rational and the non-rational course of Jewish existence wrestles with revelation all days and all nights. The great pupil of Ba'al Shem Tov, R. Jacob Joseph of Polnoy, died in 1782. In his Todot Ya'aqov Yossef he illuminates and explains tradition, Torah. And the refrain is always: 'What does sippur – history – say – bechol makom – in every place – unvechol seman – and in every age? For it is a constantly renewed faith-experience of Israel that the dynamic evolution of the word continues throughout the generations and all levels of Jewish life. Dor holech wedor ba: the generations too shall live for ever, and the world shall always be renewed. The Torah is not only revelation for Israel – it speaks to the world; but Israel is a part of revelation.

## III

The letters, words and lines of the Torah show us the dimensions of the Jewish experience of faith. We shake them up and touch the letters – everything is in the Torah. Israel too, a living commentary on Scripture, born into the covenant, constituted as a nation by the act of revelation, with its individual members who live in the covenant in belief and unbelief – bechol makom, bechol seman: witnesses of the One, the Eternal. In the polarity Israel/Torah, that means, in understanding the text, in such a way that teaching and life contend in the people, we reach a critical self-understanding in which the election of Israel becomes not self-idolatry but an everlasting task. And this compulsion to duty always leads from mystery to commandment, from the non-rational to the rational, to continuity between knowing and doing. Ernst Simon describes this as the 'sacred sobriety' of Judaism: 'The Jewish Law ordains a way of life of partial asceticism. No area of being, no fragment of the world is excluded, none is opened up without restriction. The happiness of love, pleasure in eating and drinking are not merely reluctantly permitted; they belong to God's creation for mankind. As such they are subject to his law; their due use is a religious duty, but their inappropriate use becomes transgression'.[6]

In difficult times it was possible to get lost in mystery but not permanently. Doctrine and life always found the way to one's fellow men; it was impossible to stay in the paradise of mystical speculation. That is expressly stated in the Talmud, in the Hagiga: 'Whoever speculates upon four things, what lies above, below, before and behind, it were better for him that he had never been born' (Hag. 11a).

We cannot escape from speculation but we know the dangers. Four rabbis entered the paradise of mystical contemplation: Ben Azzai, Ben Zoma, Elisha ben Abujah and Akiba. One died, one went mad, one attacked Judaism, and only Akiba entered in and made his way out peacefully. One can live in both worlds, but only if one is conscious of one's own way. The Talmud story shows this in the meeting of Joshua ben Hananiah with Ben Zoma: 'Ben Zoma saw him and did not rise before him. So the latter called out. 'Whence and whither, Ben Zoma?" And Ben Zoma answered: "I have considered the space between the upper and the lower waters; the distance between this one and that one is only three fingers... Then Reb Joshua said to his pupils: ,,Ben Zoma is still outside..." '(Hag. 15a).

Ben Zoma died soon afterwards in total confusion. But in what did his sin consist? One of the greatest teachers of his time, who was much loved and honoured, one of whom it was said after his death: 'With him the exegetes, the searchers of Holy

Writ, were buried'. Adayin Ben Zoma ba-hutz – why was he outside? Not because he discussed secret topics. The other Rabbis, in the same paragraph, treat of the same theme and disagree about the distance. Joshua saw that Ben Zoma had become unworldly. The teacher who at one time answered the question 'Who is respected?' thus: 'He who respects others', now refused to treat his colleagues with minimal courtesy. 'Who is strong?' At one time Ben Zoma taught: 'He who is in control of himself'. Whence and whither, Ben Zoma? Jewish mysticism is still conditioned by rational, ethical suasions, and Ben Zoma had taken the wrong path; he was too heavily influenced in one direction. He was outside.

Israel's way is the way of the covenant. Halakah and Haggadah, doctrine and life, the Oral and the written Law: everything comes together in the ages and lays its claim on us. And we have to listen to everything. There are many paths within the covenant, but there are also ways which lead without. If we forget that mystery leads to commandment, that Israel's covenant exists for God's covenant with mankind, then we are already outside the Torah. And if we do not proceed from commandment to mystery, as when we fall into the mundane, if dialogue with the Torah and the Law does not lead mankind into the palace of the Lawgiver, then we are outside. But we are not in the condition of the peasant in Kafka's story 'Before the Law'. We are not standing outside a door intended for us alone, but so guarded that we do not dare to enter. Many ways and many doors lead into the palace, and a critical and prudent optimism always enables us to make the attempt, again and again. Even Paul Celan, already facing death, was able gently to venture in a conversation with Nelly Sachs:

> Of your God was our talk, I spoke
> against him, I
> let the heart that I had
> hope:
> for
> his highest, death-rattled, his
> quarrelling word –[7]

It was not enough for Celan. Perhaps he was still outside. He died soon afterwards. But he and Ben Zoma, and Akiba, time and history, offer their testimony to their fellow men: it is the testimony of Israel. The Word is spoken to us, through us and to you: the Word of the Torah, the timeless revelation, which always makes a man or a woman a fellow human being. We are not only witnesses for the eternal revelation which spoke to all people on Sinai in all languages. We are witnesses for the revelation which is expressed in the life of this people of Israel through law and ritual and moral behaviour. Na-seh Venishma: our action and our knowledge are one, eternally new and old. And, should we happen to despair, when the covenant between man, the world and God lies at the farthest extremities of our existence, then, once again, we hear the word of God:

> For the mountains may depart
> and the hills be removed,
> but my steadfast love shall not depart
> from you,
> and my covenant of peace shall not be
> removed,
> says the LORD, who has compassion
> on you.
>
> (Is 54 : 10)

Leo Baeck interprets this prophetic passage thus: 'That is both law and grace for this people and for all others'.[8]

Notes

1 See E. Simon, Brücken (collected essays) (Heidelberg, 1965), p. 455.
2 Paul Celan, Poems, trans. Michael Hamburger (Manchester, 1980), p. 157.
3 Leo Baeck, Dieses Volk, Vol. I (Frankfurt am Main, 1955), pp. 20 f.
4 E. Simon, Brücken, op. cit., p. 47.
5 George Steiner, The Death of Tragedy (London, 1961), p. 6.
6 E. Simon, Brücken, op. cit., p. 468.
7 Paul Celan, Poems, op. cit., p. 133.
8 L. Baeck, Dieses Volk, Vol. I, op. cit., p. 182.

# How is Human Experience of God[1] possible in spite of strict Islamic Monotheism?

*Abdoldjavad Falaturi*

Even the bare title 'How is human experience of God possible in spite of strict Islamic monotheism?' (not only because it is cast as a question) shows that the question is a special one. We have to ask why this matter is a problem at all.

Human experience of God in Islam is a problem because in general Islamic philosophical and theological books extend the Islamic God in His absolute unity and uniqueness so far beyond all possible existential categories and so separate Him from men, that only a philosophically-trained individual can at best arrive at an abstract, rational experience of God. This kind of experience, however, can collapse at any time as a result of exploded premisses.

The Islamic experience of God is also problematic because polemical writings against Islam not infrequently object[2] that so abstract a form of monotheism is beyond the understanding of most Muslims, makes any union with God impossible, and turns it into worship of individuals and objects (stones, trees, funerary monuments and so on). Moreover, it is problematic because in Islamic conviction there is no existential ground which leads to a corresponding association with God, as is the case, for example, in Christianity with original sin and redemption (one might also cite Buddhism in this regard).

Finally, the experience of God is also problematic because the description of Islam as a religion of the Law sees man as subject to the letter of the Law, and God at best as a just ruler, and in this sense a heartless, all-powerful, forceful, angry, revengeful and unpredictably arbitrary ruler, as a terrible monster who is waiting for the arrival of the Last Day when He will finally show mankind His might: hell for you, you unfaithful creature, and paradise for you, you good and faithful servant.

The foregoing represents some of the reasons why the Islamic experience of God is problematical. In fact, to a considerable extent Islamic scholars and their works provoke such difficulties and problems. I mean philosophers, theologians, legal experts and to some dregree moralists – I exclude the Islamic mystics from the start, but I shall refer to them summarily later on.

I turn now to the founder of Islam, Muḥammad, who fortunately was not a theologian, scholar or systematic theologian, and in the Koran did not divide his teaching according to different disciplines, but focused it on the real nucleus, the experience of God.

Acquaintance with the Koran shows that the question 'How is human experience of God possible in spite of strict Islamic monotheism?' comprises not only the question but its answer. Human experience of God is assured precisely because, according to Muḥammad, what is in question is a strict monotheism: that is, the exclusion of any kind of mediator (man, nature, principle and so on) between God and man.

What does this mean?
We can arrive at an explanation of the foregoing by analyzing the three terms contained in the expression 'human experience of God', that is: God, man and experience of God.

What is God according to the Koran?
Its answer is: 'Say: 'Allāh is One, the Eternal God. He begot none, nor was He begotten. None is equal to Him'.[3] The answer regarding the rejection of God's incarnation is even clearer and more decisive: 'Nothing can be compared with Him'.[4] This kind of negative description proclaims the unity and uniqueness of God, and therefore strict monotheism, but in this form does not show how such a Being who is beyond all that is real and conceivable is to be experienced.

The quasi-anthropomorphic statements about the God of Islam are just as inadequate as answers to our problem. That he is 'the One who listens' (as-samī') and 'the seeing One' (al-basīr)[5], that he has a 'countenance' (wağh)[6], 'hand' (yad)[7] and 'throne' ('arš)[8], does not indicate that he is experienced and how he is experienced. (And of course all these expressions, which are intended to illustrate the relationship of God to his creation, are usually adjusted by Sunnite aund Shiite theologians to emphasize the perfection and absolute oneness of God.)

Even the encounter (liqā') between man and God described in the Koran is to occur only on the Day of Judgment and not in this life.[9] And yet, according to Koranic teaching, man must always have the possibility of experiencing his God, since God is always 'closer to him than the vein of his neck'.[10]

Among the essential and active characteristics which are ascribed to the God of Islam, a symbolic characterization of the existence of God and his relationship to his creation would seem to offer most proficient access to the mystery of the experience of God. What is in question is an existential illustration of divine being as offered in the Koran, of the kind which in the course of Islamic history has repeatedly engaged Islamic philosophers and mystics – less the theologians (mutakallimūn) and least of all legal experts (fuqahā᾽) – and which has permitted extremely diverse interpretations. But it is not these interpretations – which have hardly anything to do with the point at issue – but much more the Koranic answer to our problem which is of most interest. That answer is: 'Allah is the light of the heavens and the earth. His light may be compared to a niche that enshrines a lamp, the lamp within a crystal of star-like brilliance. It is lit from a blessed olive tree neither eastern nor western. Its very oil would almost shine forth, though no fire touched it. Light upon light; Allah guides to His light whom He will. Allah coins metaphors for men. He has knowledge of all things'.[11]

The following statements are important
1. Allah is light.
2. This light shines forth from itself.
3. This light is light of heaven and earth: that is, of the cosmos.
4. God offers His light to whomsoever He will.

This is certainly not light in the physical sense. In the Koran light appears similarly in another context; Torah,[12] Gospel,[13] and Koran[14] all contain light. Both applications have something in common: in content and in effect. The first light, God, is on the level of reality the really True, absolute Truth. The second, that is, light in the Torah, Gospel and Koran, is the pure Truth, truth on the level of faith: God as light from heaven and earth allows this to become apparent. The light of true faith illuminates the only right way to the One, to God.

Both kinds of light offer light of themselves, for they illuminate in their character as pure Truth per se, and not by virtue of anything else.

The statement that God is light from heaven and earth (of the universe), and the subsequent image, reassure us that no pantheism of any kind is involved here. Nor should we think of any kind of world-immanent physis. God is separate from the world and yet associated with it (transcendence and immanence at one and the same time). Hundreds of verses of the Koran describe this relationship in detail. They show that He is the only creator of heaven and earth and of all that lies between them. He is not only the creator of all that exists; He directly produces all events, occurrences and all appearances which are otherwise ascribed to men, animals, plants, earth, heaven, sun, moon, clouds, wind, rain, day, night and, in short, all other existents. Everything is to be attributed to His action and to His efficacy. Therefore He is the light of all which lies outside Him; everything appears by virtue of His light. He is not the world. But the entire universe, together with everything that is in and occurs in it, is permeated by Him. He is everywhere but He Himself is not spatial. He is always present but not temporal (if He and His activity are related to successive time, then His light is rendered transitory[15]).

Man as a part of the universe is also a work of God. His conception, birth, childhood, youth, age, waking, sleeping and all his other actions derive from God. He (God) is the one who produces all these phenomena: 'It was not you [the faithful] but Allah who slew them. It was not you [Muḥammad] who smote them: Allah smote them...'[16] This means that man too and his actions as part of the universe can occur only by virtue of the Light; through, that is, the ever-present, uniquely-effective God.

I do not need to emphasize the fact that the Koran also attributes life, knowledge, power, will and other characteristics to God constituted thus. But it is important to see how the entire work of God (man included) relates to God. In this respect the Koran says in general: 'The seven heavens, the earth, and all who dwell in them give glory to Him. All creatures celebrate His praises'.[17] Praise presupposes a certain experience of God whether one likes or not, as is confirmed in another Koranic context: 'All who dwell in the heavens and upon earth shall prostrate themselves before Allah, some willingly and some by force'.[18] The only effective God is heard, experienced, praised and petitioned[19] in His oneness and uniqueness through His work, of which man too is part, whether His creatures want this or not, whether they know it or not. This is a firm conviction to which the Koran holds with surprising consistency. Therefore: He is the only God, and therefore He alone can be experienced and addressed as such.

This is the Koranic conviction; it is based upon the notion of the reality of God as the Light that interpenetrates the entire universe.

On this foundation – and thus we come to the second question, What is man?, and the third, How does he experience God? – Light in the Torah, Gospel and Koran shows the way to another form of experience of God. It is not a genetically and existentially conditioned form of experience, and to that extent one dependent on fate, but an existential experience of God grounded on a free exercise of will.[20] Among all God's creatures, man (alongside the djinn) is pre-eminent because he – and not now God – as an active being fulfils, or can fulfil, the purpose of creation.

'I created mankind and the djinn in order that they might worship Me'.[21] The converse of this statement is: If man were not to serve God, he would not have been created. The meaning of his creation is solely that he should serve God and thus fulfil the purpose of creation.

But what does 'serve' mean here, and why should this be the meaning of creation?

What is intended is certainly not the blind subservience of an oppressed slave. Nor is service a verbal profession of Islam. Even faith in the sense of a single-minded conviction that there is one God cannot be substituted for service in this respect. Service (ᶜibāda) is rather the realization of the same light that is found in the Torah, Gospel and Koran, the fulfilment of Islam as the one, unique and true Light,[22] in other words an Islam which as the one true religion[23] was imparted to all prophets and messengers from the beginning of creation up to Muḥammad.

Hence the term ᶜabd (servant) as bearer of light, of Islam, and as the one who realizes Islam, is the most important Koranic term for man – not for man as he is, but as he ought to be according to the divine plan of creation. Adam, Abraham, Moses, David, Solomon, Jesus and Muḥammad were all ᶜabd (servants), but authentic ᶜabd. They were among those who fully realized Islam, devotion. But this realization does not occur in such lifeless actions as prayer, fasting, almsgiving, and so on, nor by fulfilling this or that moral value. The realization of devotion is ensured instead if the substance of the Light sent by God is realized only in a pure intention and righteousness (iḫlāṣ)[24] oriented to God.

To direct oneself righteously to God is a matter not only of ritual but of all human action (which is held to be a mere following of the letter of the law). Even drinking, eating, sleeping, walking, buying and everything which an ᶜabd does, is included. A true abd, who does everything in a state of righteousness directed towards God, is then not only in direct active contact (a corresponding experience) with God, with whom he is associated in destiny by virtue of his origin and his existence. An authentic abd also dwells with him (with God).[25] Accordingly, in so close a relationship (We 'are closer to him [man] than the vein in our neck'[26] ), an ᶜabd tries to win God's approval[27] in the thanksgiving which only man among all existents, for he alone apart from God acts and achieves, can offer to God.

It is not the human body but the soul, yet not the reason – rather the heart –, which is the location of such a continuing man–God relationship, an encounter with God as an experience of God. This is an experience of God which can be described neither as rational nor as empirical (as, for instance, in the case of a meeting with an individual). It is an experience of God sui generis. It is not in any way a mystical experience in the usual sense. It is a God-experience which takes place in the realization of the Light sent from God. Man, and man alone, is in a position to fulfil this goal of creation, because from the beginning the Creator made him as a creature which bears this Light, Islam, within him: 'Therefore stand firm in your devotion to the [one] true faith, the upright nature with which Allah has endowed man. Allah's creation cannot be changed. This is surely the true religion, although most men do not know it'.[28]

This means: The service, the realization of Islam, of the Light, which is grounded in the experience of God, is no redemption from an existential and fateful misfortune. It is rather the unfolding of what the Creator imparted to man, namely the unfolding of the very core of his being: that is, the unfolding of the closeness to God which is enclosed and hidden in man, the unfolding of Islam, the unfolding of surrender to the one God. This is a development which in all its stages is an authentic experience of God. One may equally describe it as a reacquisition of what was given to all men from the creation onwards, but has remained hidden from them, or as a return to the Islam which was also given them from the creation onwards. It is a question of the realization of Islam, of Light, of the devotion to the one God which is already anchored in every man. For an authentic ᶜabd it is a question of a lasting, always consonant (but not successively realized) process. This is always the experience of a God who is always present everywhere.

Of course not everyone succeeds in this fully and without error. This is shown by the example of the first man, Adam.[29] People encounter all kinds of obstacles on the way to being a true ᶜabd, on the way to finding the Light which is hidden in them. The struggle, however, the to-and-fro between God and non-God, allows a practical and living dialogue to take place between man and God. That too is an experience of God of another kind. Even in his sin, in his 'away' from God and his 'towards' non-God, man who from his creation has been endowed with divine Light, experiences his God.

If we examine in this perspective[30] the names, qualities and activities which the Koran ascribes to God, and the characteristics of man, we see that these all mark the reciprocal relationship between God and man, the only creature for whom the divine Light is intended:[31] Love, anger, reward, punishment, grace and so on on the part of the Creator, and faith, unbelief, obedience, disobedience, good, evil, repentance and so on on the part of man. Whether like this or like that, man cannot escape being affirmatively or negatively in a permanent God-experience, even if in theory or practice he rejects God.

The foregoing is not mysticism. It is a question merely of the piety emphatically recommended by the Koran (this piety, which is a necessary component of Muḥammad's teaching, was neglected by theologians and jurists satisfied with the externalities of action. It did not find its appropriate place in the division of Muḥammad's teaching into several disciplines. The steadfastness of the mystics, in seeing piety as the core of their mystical procedure, and in building upon that basis their teaching, which extended beyond the Koran, has frequently led Muslims and Islamicists to the erroneous view that piety is a mystical phenomenon). Furthermore, it is not a mystical interpretation of the Koran. However, it is not difficult for a mystic at one move to transfer the whole thing into a mystical dimension. Koranic teaching rests, as shown, on the basis of a separation between God and man as two entities. A mystic can and would (it has happened often enough in the history of Islam) remove the barrier between God and man, His favourite creature, by uniting both lights in a unio mystica: in, therefore, the self-experience of Light, precisely because here the strictest form of monotheism is involved and it is a matter of one and the same Light: the Light of heaven and earth, to which He (God) leads whomsoever He wishes.

## Notes

1 Apparently Islamic theologians and philosophers felt no need to posit the question of the possibility and reality of a human experience of God, beyond their speculations about God, the necessity of His existence and His characteristics. It is difficult even to find an appropriate Arabic or Persian expression for the experience of God, without running the danger of reducing the Islamic God in His absolute transcendence, of humanizing or reifying Him. It is therefore proper for the purposes of the present inquiry to start from the pure religious sensibility of a pious Muslim and to keep strictly to the Koran as a source, without allowing interference from the diverse opinions of various directions and schools of Islamic thought.

2 Here I am thinking especially of the discussions conducted in recent years by Christian missionaries in Islamic countries.

3 Koran, 112 : 1–4.

4 Ibid., 42 : 11.

5 Ibid., 17 : 1.

6 Ibid., 2 : 100.

7 Ibid., 5 : 64,

8 Ibid., 9 : 129.

9 Ibid., 6 : 31: 'They are lost indeed, those who deny that they will ever meet Allah'. Cf. 18 : 110.

10 Ibid., 50 : 16.

11 Ibid., 24 : 35.

12 Ibid., 5 : 44: 'There is guidance, and there is light, in the Torah which We have revealed. By it the prophets who surrendered themselves (aslamū) to Allah judged the Jews...'.

13 Ibid., 5 : 46: 'After those prophets We sent forth Jesus, the son of Mary, confirming the Torah already revealed, and gave him the Gospel, in which there is guidance and light, corroborating that which was revealed before it in the Torah, a guide and an admonition to the righteous'.

14 Ibid., 4 : 174: 'Men, you have received [through the Koranic revelation] clear evidence from your Lord. We have sent forth to you a glorious light'.

15 Cf. A. Falaturi, 'Experience of Time and History in Islam', in: We Believe in the One God, eds. A. Schimmel & A. Falaturi (London & New York, 1979), pp.63-87.

16 Koran, 8 : 17.

17 Ibid., 17 : 44.

18 Ibid., 13 : 15.

19 Praise, prostration, petitions and so on are actions which presuppose the will and awareness of the individual. Does the Koran, with its conviction that there is nothing that would not praise Him, and so on, posit a certain degree of ensoulment of the universe and that which is associated with it? If not, how should dead objects praise their Creator, and so forth? Islamic scholars have discussed this question

often and from various standpoints. There is an immanent relationship, it seems to me, between this and the other Koranic belief that everything which there is apart from God is a sign (āya) pointing to God. As the work of God, every created thing points to its Creator by reason of its existence, which depends on Him. By fulfilling the tasks allotted to it through existence, every creature demonstrates its subjection to its exalted Creator; and, through the miracle of creation, in which every created thing participates, it praises the perfection of its Lord (rabb). The Koran is able to represent this belief all the more firmly because it shows Divine Reality as a Light before human eyes, and as one which permeates the entire creation; this also implies an existential experience of God on the part of his creatures.

20 How is human free will conceivable in spite of all-inclusive divine activity? Here we are faced with one of the oldest and most difficult problems which has caused Muslims much heart-searching from the beginning. The particular resolution of this problem was the criterion for naming the first theological schools: Ǧabrīya (advocating divine compulsion) and Qadariya (advocating freedom of will).

The later schools also had to decide for or against one or the other solution, or to accept a compromise (hence the Ašʿarites and Shiites, each of course deciding in accordance with their own tenets).

The Ǧabrīya school is supported by the abovementioned Koranic belief that God is the sole effective Power, and in addition by the express confirmation: 'It was Allah who created you and all that you have made' (Koran, 37 : 96; cf. 53 : 39). The Qadariya viewpoint is supported by the human duty (constantly stressed in the Koran and in tradition) to obey commandments and prescriptions, which are followed by reward and punishment. Such a duty has to presuppose freedom of will if it is not to appear self-contradictory. But even this consideration finds support in the Koran: 'Allah does not charge a soul with more than it can bear. It shall be requited for whatever good and whatever evil it has done' (Koran, 2 : 286).

As against these two opposed theses and the Shiite and the Ašʿaritic compromise solution, the Koran itself offers yet another answer, which wholly corresponds to the God–man relationship cited here. Study of the name of God and His deeds as ascribed to Him by the Koran and tradition allows us to posit that in fact, according to Koranic belief, the uniquely powerful God is the originator of all events and actions; even actions adjudged negative are ascribed to Him, for instance He 'plots' (Koran, 2 : 54), or He 'misleads' this or that person (Koran, 44 : 88, e.g.) (without going into the theological interpretations of these and similar passages). There is, however, only one activity which by definition is excluded from God's unique activity, namely serving God, which, as already explained, constitutes the purpose of creation. Even if a convinced Muslim entertained the notion and supposed it to be possible that God should petition Himself (ʿabada nafsahū), then in contradiction to his faith he would have to maintain that the entire creation was meaningless, because on his supposition God would be able to serve Himself, which would make the creation of djinn and mankind pointless.

If, however, we allow this exception, then the fact that every man is duty-bound to service and to every action may presuppose his free will, without any contradiction. In this way the arguments of the Qadariya and Ǧabrīya are both justifiable and non-contradictory, as has been generally accepted.

For a general discussion of these points, see Montgomery Watt, Free Will and Predestination in Early Islam (London, 1948); H. Stieglecker, Die Glaubenslehren des Islam (Paderborn, 1962), pp. 97 ff.

21 Koran, 51 : 56.

22 Ibid., 39 : 22: 'He whose heart Allah has opened to Islam shall receive light from his Lord'.

23 Ibid., 3 : 19: 'The only true faith in Allah's sight is Islam'.

24 Ibid., 39 : 11: 'Say: "I am bidden to serve Allah and to worship non besides Him".' See also: 39 : 2; 39 : 14; 2 : 139; 7 : 29; 98 : 5; and so on.

[25] See ibid., 2 : 153; 5 : 11; 29 : 69; and so on.
[26] Ibid., 50 : 16.
[27] Ibid., 2 : 265.
[28] Ibid., 30 : 30.
[29] Ibid., 2 : 35–7.
[30] Under the aspect of a real relationship between God and man, and of the possibility of dialogue between man and God.
[31] If, in examining the names of God, and His essential and active characteristics, we prescind from an analysis of the relationship between God and the world as allowed by the Koran (inasmuch as, for comparison's sake, it describes God as the Light of the universe), we soon discover that every name and every characteristic of God constitutes an aspect of what the Koranic light-image says about His actual nature. For general information on this subject, see al-Asmā' al-ḥusnā in $EI^2$ I, 714 ff; G.C. Anwati, 'Un traité des noms divins', in Arabic and Islamic Studies in Honour of H.A. Gibb (Leiden, 1965), pp. 36 ff; Al-Ghazālī, al-Maqaṣad al-asnā fī šarḥ maʿānī asmāʾ Allah al-ḥusnā (Beirut, 1971).

# The Concept of Revelation in Modern Judaism

*Jakob J. Petuchowski*

A deep gulf separates man from the transcendent God of the Hebrew Bible. God is God, and man, man. The ways of God are as distant from man's ways, and God's thoughts from man's thoughts, as are the heavens from the earth. (Is. 55 : 8–9).

But this biblical attitude would never have become biblical *religion* had not recognition of the existence of this gulf been supplemented by the certainty that it can be bridged, and by the knowledge that, on occasion, the gulf *has been* bridged. This metaphor must not be misunderstood. In Judaism, the boundary lines between God and man are never obliterated. There is no apotheosis of man, and no 'incarnation' of God. But God, remaining God, makes Himself known to man, who remains man. In theology, this is called revelation.

The Bible knows of two kinds of revelation. It speaks of a 'vision' or 'sight',[1] and it speaks of 'the Word of the Lord'[2] or 'Torah',[3] the divine guidance. Rabbinic Judaism was, therefore, faithful to its biblical prototype when, instead of using an ambiguous term like 'revelation', it spoke, as the occasions demanded, either of gilluy shekhinah (the revealing of God's presence) or of mattan torah (the gift of divine guidance).

For Rabbinic Judaism, as is well known, the Pentateuch was the document of revelation par excellence. It possessed a greater degree of authority than the Prophets and the Hagiographa. But, contrary to what might have been expected, this authority of the Pentateuch did not lead the Rabbis to espouse a literalist fundamentalism. The same Rabbis who had elevated the Pentateuch to the position of highest authority in questions of belief and practice nevertheless insisted that the totality of God's revelation was not confined to the Pentateuch – not to the Pentateuch, and not even to the Bible as a whole.

The Rabbis taught the dogma of the 'twofold revelation'. In addition to the Written Torah, which God gave to Moses in the form of the Pentateuch, He also revealed an Oral Torah, which alone provides a complete understanding of the Written Torah. One could compare this with the role which tradition plays in the Roman Catholic Church, or with the hadith in Islam.

This Oral Torah, transmitted by masters to disciples through the generations, was actually never meant to be fixed in written form. It was only in later centuries, motivated by the fear the 'the Torah will be forgotten in Israel', that the Rabbis dared to set aside the prohibition of committing the Oral Torah to writing. Thus there came into existence the written works of the Talmud and the Midrashim. But even the many volumes of that literature do not claim to contain the totality of God's revelation. The Talmud itself reports discussions about the question whether the greater part of the Torah was given in writing or orally. Later Judaism seems to have accepted Rabbi Yohanan's answer: 'The greater part of the Torah was given orally, and only the smaller part was given in writing'.[4]

It is the totality of the Torah, in its written and in its oral components, which is meant by the statement of the Mishnah: 'Moses received the Torah at Sinai, and transmitted it to Joshua. Joshua transmitted it to the elders, the elders to the Prophets, and the Prophets to the Men of the Synagoga Magna'.[5] The latter, in their turn, transmitted the Torah to the first heads of the Rabbinic academies.

This was a *dogmatic* formulation, not an attempt to write history. For, in the first place, the Pentateuch itself contains reports about legislation enacted both before and after the Sinaitic Revelation. And then there actually are differences of opinion expressed in the Talmud as to whether the Torah was given in a series of separate scrolls, or whether it was given as a complete and self-contained document. Both points of view are represented in the Talmud. Neither was pronounced heretical.[6] Moreover, the Rabbinic sources quite openly admit that various laws and institutions of the Oral Torah are of human origin. Indeed, they report the specific historical conditions, long after the Sinaitic Revelation, which were responsible for the origin of such laws and institutions.

For example, the kindling of the Hanukkah lights on the Feast of the Maccabees is not only a component of the Oral Torah, but it is also an observance for which the Oral Torah ordains the following benediction (berakhah): 'Blessed art Thou, O Lord, our God, Sovereign of the Universe, who hast sanctified us through

Thy commandments, and commanded us to kindle the light of Ḥanukkah'. The Rabbis were fully conscious of the fact that the Feast of Hanukkah did not go back to the Sinaitic Revelation, and that the Hasmoneans in the second century BCE introduced that festival. Nevertheless, the Rabbis found in the seventeenth chapter of the Book of Deuteronomy the legitimization for the Hasmoneans to ordain the kindling of the Ḥanukkah lights. In this way, they connected an innovation of the second century BCE with the Sinaitic Revelation.[7]

But that is history – history which was never denied, even at the time when the *dogma* was promulgated that the *whole* Torah originated at Sinai. For the 'gift of the Torah' was a concept, a generalization which was independent of any single historical event.[8]

The *divine* origin of the Torah, both written and oral, that, and only that, was elevated to the position of a dogma. As long as one believed in that divine origin, one was permitted to argue about the 'how' and the 'when'. That is why the Rabbis had no dogma about the *Mosaic* authorship of the Pentateuch, even though they accepted that authorship as an historical fact, but not as a dogma. Only the last few verses of Deuteronomy, describing the death and the burial of Moses, came, according to the view of some of the Rabbis, from the pen of Joshua.[9]

However, if revelation means the bridging of the gulf between God and man, it is to be expected that both parties share in this process. The biblical paradigm of revelation is ascending man and descending God. Thus it is indeed described in the nineteenth chapter of the Book of Exodus. In the third verse, we read: 'And Moses went up to God'. And the twentieth verse says: 'And the Lord descended upon Mount Sinai'. This daring picture becomes even more daring in Rabbinic literature, where Moses is depicted as some kind of Prometheus who wrests the Torah from the hands of the angels; indeed, some passages even assert that Moses struggled for possession of the Torah with God Himself.[10]

Perhaps it was in order to counteract such daring imagery that Rabbi José asserted: 'The shekhinah (God's Presence) never descended to earth, and Moses and Elijah never ascended to heaven.'[11] But even if one accepts the daring pictures, the thought that man is capable of receiving the revelation of God remains a thought which seems to be contradicted by normal experience.

'Rabbi Azariah and Rabbi Aḥa said in the name of Rabbi Yoḥanan: "When Israel heard the first word of the Ten Commandments at Sinai, their soul fled away... The word returned to the Holy One, praised be He, and spoke: 'Sovereign of the Universe, Thou livest forever, and Thy Torah liveth forever. But Thou hast sent me to the dead. They are all dead!" Then God made the word more palatable'.

'Rabbi Simeon bar Yoḥai taught: "The Torah, which the Holy One, praised be He, gave to Israel, restored their soul to them. That is why it is written in Psalm 19 : 8: 'The Torah of the Lord is perfect, restoring the soul'."[12]

The Word of God can kill as well as revive. In order to accomplish the latter, the Rabbis seem to teach in the passages just quoted, the Word of God must be adapted to the human condition.

This cooperation between the divine and the human and this freedom vis-à-vis the letter remained characteristic, too, of medieval Judaism. It also preserved modern Judaism from many conflicts with the modern view of the world. One should ponder, for example, Rabbi Solomon ben Isaac's comment on the first chapter of Genesis. That eleventh-century exegete of Bible and Talmud quite soberly remarked: 'This passage of Scripture does not have the purpose of instructing us concerning the chronological sequence of creation'. One should think of the words of Maimonides, who, in the twelfth century, asserted: 'The gates of interpretation are never closed'[17], and who demanded that the meaning of the Scriptural word should always be in harmony with science and philosophy. There is, after all, only *one* Source of Truth, in which both Scripture and philosophy originated.

Indeed, Judaism was preserved from many conflicts with the modern world to which other religious systems were exposed. But not from *every* conflict. The concern of the nineteenth century was not only with biblical literalism and the Darwinian theory of evolution, with miracles and with anthropomorphism. With all of that, Jewish Orthodoxy could deal on a purely traditionalist basis. All one has to do is to look at the commentary on the Pentateuch by the late Joseph Herman Hertz. Hertz was the Orthodox Chief Rabbi of England.

The real problem existed on another level or, rather, on two other levels. First of all, modern biblical criticism denied the Mosaic authorship of the Pentateuch. As we have already seen, the Mosaic authorship of the Pentateuch per se was no dogma of Talmudic Judaism, although Maimonides, in the twelfth century, had designated it as such. But Maimonides himself did not possess the authority to promulgate dogmas which had to be accepted by the whole of Jewry. In spite of this, nineteenth-century Jewish Orthodoxy felt threatened by modern biblical criticism.

Perhaps not the least reason for this was the fact that Reform Judaism, born in the nineteenth century, saw in the denial of the Mosaic authorship of the Pentateuch a justification for its denial of the authority of the Law. This, of course, was no logical necessity. After all, God could have made known His will to the Deuteronomist, to the authors of the Priestly Code, and so on, in very much the same way in which, according to the older view, He had made it known to Moses. But that was hardly the point made by the Reformers. Even before the fashion arose of distinguishing the various 'sources' of the Pentateuch, Reform Judaism had striven for a loosening of the bonds of the so-called 'ceremonial law'. Now it welcomed modern biblical scholarship as a support in the battle against the inconvenient observances of the ancestors. If Moses did not write the Pentateuch, then the Bible and the Talmud, which was based on the Bible, have lost their authority for us! In addition to that, Judaism's ability to evolve, Reform Judaism's main claim, seemed to have been demonstrated by modern biblical scholarship even for the biblical period itself.

Jewish Orthodoxy reacted to this in a twofold manner. In some circles, modern biblical scholarship was simply rejected on dogmatic grounds. A Frankfurt rabbi, Samson Raphael Hirsch (1808-1888), asserted that the methods of literary criticism could be applied to human documents only. But the Torah is a *divine* document, inaccessible to those methods. In other circles, the attempt was made to refute biblical criticism on scientific grounds. For example, David Hoffmann (1843-1921), the Director of the Orthodox Rabbinical Seminary in Berlin, published his book, Die wichtigsten Instanzen gegen die Graf-Wellhausensche Hypothese ('The Most Important Arguments against the Graf-Wellhausen Hypothesis'), in 1904. To this day, Jewish Orthodoxy has retained those two belligerent positions. Nor has Reform Judaism, on the whole, departed from its position in this matter.

Only Franz Rosenzweig (1886-1929), who stood above all parties, was able to point to a new way: 'For us, too', he wrote in 1927, 'the Torah is the work of one spirit. We do not know who it was. We cannot believe that it was Moses. Among ourselves, we call him by the sign with which critical scholarship designates the final redactor, whose existence it assumes: R. But we do not resolve this R into "redactor", but into Rabbenu ("our Master"). For, whoever he was, and whatever may have been in front of him, he is our Master, and his theology is our Teaching'.[14]

As I have said, Reform Judaism has not yet moved from its espousal of biblical criticism and from the practical consequence which it derived from it at the end of the nineteenth century. But it should be noted that, especially since the Second World War, an ever-increasing number of younger theologians of Reform Judaism has adopted the view of Rosenzweig. They see in biblical criticism a great help in the understanding of the *literary* history of the Bible. But, as far as *belief* in revelation is concerned, the findings of biblical criticism can be adduced neither for it nor against it.

With that, we have reached the second level of the modern conflict. Revelation, in the biblical and in the Rabbinic sense, meant the bridging of the gulf between the transcendent God and man. But that transcendent God no longer fared so well in the days of Hegel. He became an immanent Absolute, and proud man self-consciously became His bearer. Such a God does not reveal Himself to man – neither from above nor from outside. The very basis of the biblical concept of revelation had now disappeared.

As a consequence, modern Judaism, too, twisted revelation into inspiration. Shakespeare, Goethe and Bach had been inspired. No doubt, so were Isaiah and Jeremiah; and, if he existed at all, Moses, too.

'What is revelation?', Schleiermacher asked; and he answered his own question: 'Every original and new communication of the Universe to man is a revelation, as, for example, every... moment of conscious insight...'[15].

With that kind of 'revelation' one could come to terms in the nineteenth century. One could even find points of contact with certain rationalistic tendencies in medieval Jewish philosophy, and subscribe to the thesis advanced by the radical Reform rabbi, David Einhorn (1809-1870): 'After all this, the more recent form of Judaism is simply logically more consistent, when it refuses to regard revelation as something external, but rather views Reason, the rational breath of God within man, as revelation's sole agent with respect to all *truths and laws* of Judaism. In the case of the Prophet, Reason possesses an *extraordinary*, but by no means a *supernatural* degree of development and divine enlightenment, which enables the Prophet to be ahead of other men by centuries and even millennia.'[16]

But what happens if, in spite of one's rejection of the concrete, biblical concept of revelation, one wants to hang on to positive religion? That, after all, was also a concern of the thinkers of Reform Judaism. In their striving for emancipation and adaptation, they may have sacrificed many customs and observances which were uniquely Jewish; but they still wanted to remain Jews. In order to accomplish this, they now relied upon a theory of revelation, which, contrary to all of their other striving, stressed the biologico-national aspect of the Jewish character. Abraham Geiger (1810-1874), the pioneer of Reform Jewish theology, understood revelation as the special Jewish genius for religion![17]

But Kaufmann Kohler (1843-1926), *the* theologian of "classical" American Reform Judaism, wrote in 1910: 'It is an indisputable fact of history that the Jewish people, on account of its peculiar religious bent, was predestined to be the people of revelation. Its leading spirits, its prophets and psalmists, its law-givers and inspired writers differ from the seers, singers, and sages of other nations by their unique and profound insight into the moral nature of the Deity.'[18]

Kohler apparently never realized that, in making this statement, he had moved into spiritual proximity to the Zionist thinker, Asher Ginzberg (1856-1927), known as Ahad Ha'Am. On the contrary, he even pointed out that 'Asher Ginzberg and the rest of the nationalists underrate the religious power of the Jew's soul'.[19] Kohler also lacked the insight which was expressed some years ago by Emil Fackenheim: 'If we Jews have indeed produced religious genius, we have given it, long ago, to the world; we cannot and dare not keep its insights to ourselves. We try in vain to save Jewish religious particularism on non-supernatural grounds; in the end, we are led to a perversion of classical Jewish doctrine: the substitution, for the worship of God, of thc worship of the "Jewish vision" of God.'[20]

Even Leo Baeck (1873-1956) still tried, in his treatment of revelation, to avoid the supernatural. Ethical monotheism, for him, was indeed a 'revolution'. This monotheism, according to Baeck, did not slowly evolve out of polytheism, 'for there never has been any development of a *nature religion*... into an *ethical religion* in which God is something other than natural, in which He is the Holy One, the originator of morality, who is worshipped in the right deed alone'.[21] The 'One God' of Israel is, for Baeck, 'the *first word* of a *new* way of thinking'. That is why Baeck feels justified, 'historically', as he says, 'disregarding first of all every supernatural interpretation', in calling this form of religion, 'a *revelation'*.[22]

As long as man still proudly stalked the earth as a particle of the Absolute, as long as philosophical Idealism still ruled minds, one could indeed disregard every supernatural interpretation. But times have changed. The world has become different. Once again, man sees himself as *only* man – with all of the existential consequences which follow from this. The immanent God of the nineteenth century has either been dissolved in atheistic Existentialism or replaced, in religious Existentialism, by 'The Wholly Other', the transcendent God.

The religious person of today thus finds himself or herself again in the situation of biblical man: God is God, and man is man. May we conclude from this that the biblical concept of revelation, which, at one time, arose in a similar situation, has likewise become accessible again to people of today? Precisely that is the problem which must occupy modern Jewish theology.

Of course, this theology cannot cease being 'modern'. There can be no thought of denying the scientific results of biblical criticism. The documents of revelation will continue to be viewed as human documents. The laws and institutions, which claim to be grounded in revelation, will continue to be regarded as human laws and as human institutions. But the objection which Karl Jaspers once raised against Rudolf Bultmann, 'I do not understand how you can regard something human as the word of God,'[23] is an objection to which modern Jewish theology will reply by pointing to an external, divine cause as the origin of that which happens within the human being.

That is why, for example, Martin Buber (1878-1965) could write: 'My own belief in revelation... does not mean that I believe that finished statements about God were handed down from heaven to earth. Rather it means that the human substance is melted by the spiritual fire which visits it, and there now breaks forth from it a word, a statement, which is human in its meaning and form, human conception and human speech, and yet witnesses to Him who stimulated it and to His will.'[24]

Already, eighteen hundred years before Martin Buber, Rabbi

Ishmael taught: 'The Torah speaks in the language of the children of man'.[25] In the nineteenth century, it might have been forgotten that, behind the language of the children of man, there still was the Torah. Today, the attempt is made to rediscover the Torah, God's self-revelation, behind the language of the children of man. It is the great merit of Franz Rosenzweig that, in this rediscovery, he has shown the way to many modern Jewish theologians. Lack of space prevents me from giving an exposition of Rosenzweig's philosophy of revelation. But I should like to conclude my contribution with this quotation from Franz Rosenzweig: 'If one tells a tale about Hansel and Gretel, it need only be pretty. Neither the witch nor the parents are going to raise an objection about being misrepresented – for they really do not exist at all. But if one wants to tell a tale about God's revelation, it becomes a far more ticklish business. Here it does not suffice that the story should be pretty; it must also be true. Otherwise one runs the danger of having God raise an objection. For, unlike the witch and the parents, God *does* exist. He cannot be indifferent to the kind of tales His children tell about Him – any less than He can be indifferent to the name by which they call Him. Yet they remain tales; and you need not worry that research into literary history will be robbed of a subject matter. All narrative, as such, turns into a tale. That is human. And God wants the human – also in His own revelation.'[26]

## Notes

1 Ex. 3 : 1 ff; Ez. 11 : 24; Hos. 12 : 11; and frequently in the Bible.
2 Deut. 5 : 5 and frequently.
3 Is. 2 : 3 and frequently. Cf. Jakob J. Petuchowski, Ever Since Sinai – A Modern View of Torah (Milwaukee, [3]1979), pp.4–12.
4 B. Gittin 60b.
5 Mishnah Abhoth 1 : 1.
6 B. Gittin 60a.
7 B. Shabbath 23a. Cf. Jakob J. Petuchowski, Heirs of the Pharisees (New York, 1970), pp. 61–4.
8 Cf. Max Kadushin, The Rabbinic Mind (New York, [2]1965), pp. 57 f.
9 Cf. Jakob J. Petuchowski, 'The Supposed Dogma of the Mosaic Authorship of the Pentateuch', in: The Hibbert Journal, Vol. 57 (1959), pp. 356-60.
10 Cf. Louis Ginzberg, The Legends of the Jews, Vol. III (Philadelphia, 1911), pp. 109–14.
11 B. Sukkah 5a.
12 Midrash Shir Hashirim Rabbah 6 : 3.
13 Moses Maimonides, Moreh Nebhukhim, II, 25.

[14] Franz Rosenzweig , Briefe, ed. Ernst Simon (Berlin, 1935), p. 582.

[15] Friedrich Schleiermacher, On Religion – Speeches to Its Cultured Despisers, trans. John Oman (New York, 1958), p. 89.

[16] David Einhorn, 'Prinzipielle Differenzpunkte zwischen altem und neuem Judenthume', in: Sinai, Vol. II (Baltimore, 1857), p. 401.

[17] Cf. Abraham Geiger, Judaism and Its History, trans. Maurice Mayer (New York, 1865), pp. 47–64.

[18] Kaufmann Kohler, Grundriss einer systematischen Theologie des Judentums (Berlin, 1910); ET: Jewish Theology (New York, 1918), pp. 38 f.

[19] Kohler, op. cit., p. 7n.

[20] Emil L. Fackenheim, Quest for Past and Future (Bloomington, 1968), p. 72.

[21] Leo Baeck, The Essence of Judaism, trans. Victor Grubwieser & Leonard Pearl (London, 1936), p. 53.

[22] Baeck, loc. cit.

[23] Karl Jaspers & Rudolf Bultmann, Myth and Christianity (New York, 1958), p. 81.

[24] Martin Buber, Eclipse of God (New York, 1952), pp. 173 f.

[25] B. Berakhoth 31b and frequently in Rabbinic literature.

[26] Rosenzweig, op. cit., p. 537.

# The 'Imitation of God' in Judaism

*Michael Brocke*

*'You shall be holy;*
*for I the Lord your God am holy' (Lev. 19 : 2).*
*'To whom then will you compare me,*
*that I should be like him? says the Holy One (Is. 40 : 25).*
*'Thou meetest those who work righteousness,*
*those that remember thee in thy ways' (Is. 64 : 4)*[1].

Only a few decades ago every Jewish community, large or small, supported a considerable number of associations, fraternities, and foundations of all kinds: religious, philanthropic, and so on. The same is true of some communities today. The majority of these 'initiatives' were or are dedicated to social tasks and services which people nowadays expect the welfare state to provide for them.

These organizations always bore and bear more or less the same traditional names: Ṣedaqa (righeousness, almsgiving = general almsgiving); Malbish'arumim (clothing the naked); Biqqur ḥolim (visiting the sick); Hakhnassat oreḥim (hospitality to travellers); Hakhnassat kalla (dowries and clothing for brides); Gemilut ḥessed (welfare, meaning here for the most part financial aid by means of interest-free loans); and the Ḥevra Qadisha (the sacred association = the burial society).

As good an example as any is a smaller German community, Regensburg in 1933 (with 81,106 inhabitants, of whom 427 were Jews): four central welfare organizations: the 'Ḥevra Qadisha' for men and one for women; the second was also concerned with 'Biqqur ḥolim', especially care of children in hospital, and financed convalescent holidays for the less advantaged. Thirdly, there was a 'Hakhnassat Oreḥim' for Jewish travellers and salesmen, and fourthly the general welfare organization 'Ṣedaqa'. These were several other foundations, one of them for 'Hakhnassat kalla': providing dowries and clothing for poor brides.[2]

Perhaps this description of Jewish welfare will seem somewhat inapposite to a religious-historical survey of the concept of imitation of God. It serves however to avoid the conscious or unconscious error of supposing what I have to say hereafter to be an anhistorical theologoumenon, or one without any practical relevance.

Imitation is actual human practice and sacrifice in accordance with a model. That is how it is understood in Judaism and therefore becomes a not unproblematical theme, though it is still only a partial aspect of the question of the relationship between God and man, and there is no unambiguous abstract term in Hebrew for imitatio dei.[3]

Certainly the biblical notion of imitation developed in early Judaism under strong Greek influence, yet it is impossible first to describe it as problematical in regard to biblical tradition and Judaism, and then, on account of a large number of Jewish citations and exegetical references, to see it as 'apparently inappropriately omitted from Judaism'.[4]

Imitation as following, or walking in the paths of God, does not appear in Scripture. Anyone who tries to find it there is working from other premisses, which are inappropriate to this context. Imitation of God is seldom explicitly required in the Bible and only briefly referred to, for instance in Deut. 15 : 12–5, where the liberation of slaves is called for with a reference to the divine redemption of Israel from Egypt, or Deut. 10 : 16–6: foreigners are to be loved because (a) God loves them and (b) the people of Israel were themselves foreigners. Hence the inclusive commandment of consecration becomes all the more significant (Lev. 11 : 44–6 and 19 : 2).

A culture and religion like Judaism which is existentially orientated and directed to its Scripture will nevertheless discover implicit references to imitation and try continually to obtain new insights from the paradox that the Bible is able to say that God is a 'consuming fire' and at the same time that one should 'hold fast to him' (Deut. 4). This paradox, on which a hundred variations are made and can be made, is something verifiable in all the religious traditions represented here.

First we must ask how in the course of its history Israel maintained and made historically effective the dialectic of the absolute unattainability of God and the most intimate dependency on him, of the *commandment* to love and the *injunction* against making an image of him.

A second necessary question is: Are the popular, pragmatic and unsystematic pronouncements of post-biblical Judaism about the imitation of God still applicable and relevant today, or are they rather naive or outdated expressions of a pre-critical religious consciousness?

But if the paradox of the imitation yet inaccessibility of God applies not only to Judaism but to those religions represented in our ecumenical colloquium, the question relates not only to the power, significance or inadequacy of the imitation of God in present-day Judaism, but to associated or daughter religions (even though that is somewhat outside the framework of my deliberations).

How did Judaism become convinced that it was possible to imitate God withouth absurdity or presumption?

Biblically speaking, it is painfully clear how partial and fragmentary the imitation of God must be. The fact that man is made in God's image and likeness (Gen. 1 : 26 f) has no consequence in this regard; to wish to imitate the Creator of worlds, to work such miracles as the liberation from Egypt, to raise the dead, would be not only presumptuous but ridiculous. Where, then, is the specifically divine element of human imitation of God?

How, in view of the foregoing, is it possible to reach the certainty of Judaism that God requires us to imitate Him, indeed that He longs for us to do so, and hence that imitatio dei is an essential characteristic of Judaism?

The possibility of the imitation of God is in fact to be found in the Bible, in an area of life where the contradictions of inaccessibility and approachability are unmistakable.

In Ex. 33 Moses addresses two requests to God: '...show me thy glory' (v. 18), and: '... show me now thy ways' (v. 13). The request to see the glory of God is rejected: '...man shall not see me and live' (v. 20). Detailed information is given, however, about the 'ways' in 34 : 6 ff, preceded by a short reference in v. 19. God wants 'to make all his goodness' pass before Moses. Thus Moses learns:

6 'The Lord passed before him, and proclaimed: "The Lord, the Lord, a God merciful and gracious, slow to anger, and abounding in steadfast love and faithfulness,
7 keeping steadfast love for thousands, forgiving iniquity and transgression and sin,

but who will by no means clear the guilty,
visiting the iniquity of the fathers upon the children and
the children's children, to the third and the fourth generation".
8 And Moses made haste to bow his head towards the earth...
9 And he said: "If now I have found favour in thy sight, O Lord,
let the Lord, I pray thee, go in the midst of us, although it is
a stiff-necked people; and pardon our iniquity and our sin, and
take us for thy inheritance".'

In this difficult text and context, Jewish tradition discerns the revelation of the 'thirteen Middōt' (measurements, characteristics, or modes of behaviour) of God. They define the area within which imitation can occur. The traditors of the Torah feel no strain in that this list of God's Middōt also contains negative elements: 'who will by no means clear the guilty' and so on. In liturgical usage the negative aspect is intentionally omitted. The Hebrew allows it to break off in v. 7a in the middle of the infinitive construction and to close significantly 'who will clear!' The following element (7b–9a) is omitted and the closing passage is 9b: 'And pardon our iniquity and sin, and take us for thy inheritance'.[5]

The we-petition of 9b shows clearly enough that there is full awareness of the possibility that God will punish 'to the third and the fourth generation'. The intention here is to stress that God's behaviour is imitable and that the 'ways of God' may be followed by men, yet at the same time to make clear that the ways of God are not like the ways of men: that is, man is not equipped to imitate all the characteristics ascribed to God. Raḥum veḥanun, merciful and gracious, slow to anger, forgiving– that is the 'way' of God. But the ways of God are not to be discovered among the errors and confusion of mortals; rather they are imparted by God Himself in the Torah and through the prophets and Scripture.

We do not know when the 'characteristics' named in Ex.34 : 6ff were extended beyond the indicative 'Show me thy ways' (Ex. 33 : 13) and equated with the 'ways of God' often cited in the Bible – which are: 'steadfast', 'gracious', 'favourable' and 'holy' (Ps. 77). It is an equation which means that wherever God's 'ways' are mentioned, his Middōt can come to mind and not his commandments (Miṣwot).

Perhaps Deut. 11 : 27 will make my point clearer: 'For if you will be careful to do all this commandment which I command you to do, loving the Lord your God, walking in all his ways, and cleaving to him...' For us this is a superfluous, ultimately synonymous statement which we would class as redundant. But Israel studied it and tried to understand what the various elements of the sentence might mean. It perceived that the 'ways' were not merely to be equated with the 'commandments', but knew that in the case of God's 'ways' it was summoned to 'walk in all God's ways', that is, to imitate Him.

The most specific summons to imitation precedes a longer list of proscriptions and commandments in Lev. 19: 'You shall be holy; for I the Lord your God am holy' (v. 2). God is holy; therefore Israel should be holy. This consecration is explained in what follows. The old meaning of 'set apart' retained in qadosh – holy – is clearly revealed when the commandments predominate, and for us today 'worship' and ethos are confused. Therefore we cannot construct a positive ethics on the basis of this summons to imitatio; this solution[6] however is inadequate, for here we find not only prohibitions but recommendations, and the commandment of love of one's neighbour is at the centre of the chapter. Nevertheless, this apparently so ill-arranged text, seemingly jumbling together major and minor themes, shows that God is a hidden and concealing God whose holiness remains absolute, whether Israel consecrates itself and thereby glorifies him or not.[7] Hence the injunction to be holy does not mean 'Be holy *just as* I am holy, but affirms that it *is* possible to be holy. Moreover Judaism gradually allows all modes of behaviour that are pronounced by God and required of man to be assumed into the concept 'holy', so that God is the one who is holy in a wealth of things holy. Accordingly Maimonides saw the injunction to be holy of Lev. 19 : 2 not as a single commandment to be included among the six hundred and thirteen commandments of things to be done and things not to be done, but a commandment to fulfil all the commandments.[8]

Once we have identified the 'ways' of God with his Middṓt, as in Lev. 19, many statements in Scripture may be understood as treating of imitation and as referring to it. Yet rabbinical exegesis does not restrict its homiletic inducements to imitation to the foregoing citations. Far beyond the express scriptural injunctions to do something because God does it (or is it), both the scripturally exact and free exegesis and eisegesis of Jewish teachers find hints on how man can imitate God: whether God definitely behaves as man ought to behave, or God behaves in a way quite different from that which is conventional for 'flesh and blood' in this or that group or convention.

The following texts show clearly that the Jewish mode of imitation of God is directed primarily to ethical and practical activity.

The texts themselves are difficult to date. This is an old problem which has hardly been brought any nearer to solution, and is acknowledged to be difficult. But since there are quite satisfactorily datable references to imitation in Matthew (5 : 48) and Luke (6 : 36), we should take advantage of them, while guarding against the error of playing off these Jewish testimonies against other Jewish testimonies which have no authorial names behind them, or were recorded only at a later time.

The exemplification of the imitability of God raises the problem of anthropomorphism. The question whether Scripture is especially aware of the problem of anthropomorphic statements about God may be left aside. But, even in its anti-anthropomorphic discourse, it is influenced by anthropomorphism. The post-biblical rabbinical period goes a little further in this regard, but not so far as to try to avoid anthropomorphisms in general. If anything, it overdoes them not qualitatively but quantitatively. The delight in contrastive theologoumena and certainly the necessity (conditioned by circumstances of the time) to take statements about high and low, incomparability and similarity, in regard to God to an extreme, cannot avoid anthropomorphism. The descriptions of the relations of God and Israel are bold, though they might have counterweights in rabbinical positions which stress God's absolute, transcendent, unrelated nature, or not. It would be wrong systematically to codify the selected texts, especially since there is no Jewish theology in the systematic sense. That does not mean that these texts are only non-obligatory (in the legal sense, they may be 'unbinding'). In Jewish moral literature and ethics to the present, they are called on before all else, when it is necessary to decide exactly what imitation of God means.

Post-biblical Jewish teaching on imitation begins, as far as one is able to determine, with the exposition of a verse of the 'Victory Hymn on the Seashore': zeʾeli weʾanwehu – 'This is my God and I will *praise* him (Ex. 15 : 2). The word anwehu (a hapaxlegoumenon) offers difficulties. In Mechilta Shira 3 it is variously interpreted by several Tannaitic scholars. Abba Saul (c. 150) takes it to be ani wehu = I and He, and interprets thus: 'I will be like unto Him (or: Be like unto Him), just as He is merciful and gracious, so must you too be merciful and gracious!' The introduction varies according to each of the several readings in which the foregoing appears anonymously or under other names. The sentence 'just as He... so must you' remains the same, whether following the introduction appropriately (*I* will; *you* should; let *us*). It appears to be a formula, a figure of speech which may be older than the first name with which it is connected.[9]

The following group of texts represents God as the ethical Actor who Himself teaches men how to behave morally, because He is not only a 'layer down of norms' but Himself does what He requires and shows men in human action what that is.

The targumim or Targums, translations of the liturgical Torah readings into vernacular Aramaic, sometimes go so far as to explain the biblical text, inserting paraphrases and extensions, in accordance with their popular-parenetic nature. Hence the Palestine Targums insert accounts of works of mercy (gemilut ḥessed), performed by God Himself, on different occasions, in Gen. 35 : 9 when Jacob mourns over Rebekah or her nurse or at the death of Moses (Deut. 34 : 6).[10]

Jacob mourns in Gen. 35 : 8, and the next verse tells of God appearing and blessing him. God taught (the Targumist seizes this opportunity to relate) the bride and bridegroom to adorn themselves, for He introduced Eve to Adam. He taught that the sick should be visited, as He visited Abraham when the latter was ill as a result of circumcision in old age (a Haggadic derivation from the union of Gen. 17 : 24 and 18 : 1). Here He teaches that mourners should be comforted just as He comforted Jacob.

The homily at the death of Moses in Deut. 34 : 6 is more detailed. God's pedagogically exemplary good deeds begin with the clothing of the naked (the garments of skins for Adam and Eve in Gen. 3 : 21), and proceeds by way of the bringing together of bride and bridegroom (Gen. 2 : 21), visiting the sick (Gen. 18 : 1), the comforting of the mourner (Gen. 35 : 9), and the feeding of the hungry (Ex. 16 : 4, with manna, that is, not by God 'personally') up to the burial of the dead, where Deut. 34 : 5 in the Bible reads: 'So Moses... died... and he buried him in the valley...' Who? – God himself buried him.

These series were certainly not manufactured by the Targumist, but were borrowed from existing individual interpretations and attached as required, with varying extents, at suitable points. There is nothing to persuade us that the basic content of this haggadōt appeared only after AD 135. What is said is very plain: Treat your neighbour just as God behaved 'in a highly personal way' in history 'from Adam to Moses', and has acted in human life right up to death.

A resumption of a similar chain that we can date later (third century) connects it with the paradox that God is described in Scripture as a 'consuming fire', yet we must follow and cleave to Him. The contradiction disappears in the middṓt, the effective ways of God in which man can 'walk': 'The Holy One, may He be praised, visited the sick... so may you also visit the sick... comforted mourners... so may you also comfort mourners...'[11]. It does not mean that God visited a sick person, comforted a mourner, buried a dead man, but visited sick people, comforted mourners, buried the dead. Assuredly He did all that to the great figures of the great past, yet He acts similarly in the present.[12]

A Tannaitic passage, by creatively associating two scriptural citations, equates the ways of God, both his middṓt and his names: Deut. 11 : 22: '...walking in all his ways'. These are the ways of God: 'God, a merciful and gracious God' (Ex. 34 : 6) and 'All who are called with the name of the Lord will be delivered' (Joel 2 : 30; reading yiqqareʾ instead of yiqraʾ) – But how is it possible for man to be called by the name of God?! Rather: God is called merciful – may you too be merciful. The Holy One, may He be praised, is called gracious – may you too be gracious. As it is written: 'God is gracious (ḥanun) and merciful' (Ps. 145 : 8) and may you too give alms gratis (ḥinam). God is called righteous, as it is written: 'For God is righteous (ṣadiq), He loves Ṣedaqot (= examples of righteousness, almsgiving)' (Ps. 11 : 7) – may you too be righteous (ṣadiq). God is called ḥassid, as it is written: (Jer. 3 : 12): 'For I am ḥassid says the Lord...' may you too be ḥassid. Therefore it is written: (Joel 3 : 5) 'All who are called with the name of the Lord will be delivered...'[13]

The same source offers, in regard to Deut. 11 : 22, another, somewhat odd way of resolving the impossibility of 'cleaving' to the 'fire': '... rather: cleave to the learned and the disciples of scholars', God looks on this as if man 'were elevated to the heights'.[14] This statement is interesting because, by its acceptance, for example, into the 'Book of Commandments' (under positive commandment number six, Rabbi Moshe ben Maimon offers: ‘by marrying the daughter of a scholar to cleave to the Shekhina’ ) under late Hassidism, it also offered the humblest Jew by virtue of cleaving to the ‘Zaddik’, a charismatic ‘righteous man’ of holy character, the possibility of cleaving to God.[15]

Reference to the ways of God in regard to imitation enables the Jew who lives by Scripture not to forget that a perfect imitatio dei is impossible, and that what it really comes to is his choice of these ‘ways’.[16]

God’s biblical ‘jealousy’ and ‘anger’ show that God rules over jealousy, not jealousy over him; the converse is true for man, who may not imitate these divine characteristics.[17]

For the Haggadah God’s example is always a positive ethical model. For negative injunctions, which are associated with consecration, midrash does not use the personal model of God.

On the other hand there is a great number of haggadic texts – especially similes – which do not aim directly at imitation of God but instead indirectly instruct the hearer not to behave in conformity with the ‘way of the world’. Such texts compare the behaviour of God with that of ‘flesh and blood’ and confirm the difference between God’s action, favourable to mankind, and the usual characteristics of earthly rulers or men in general. God, so one of these similes says, is like a king who is willing himself to pay tribute, even though all tributes belong to him.[18]

God is above the conditions of rule and the conventions of this world – to cite such a comparison of all possibilities is a significant achievement of the rabbinic teachers which contributed to the everyday inculcation of the imitation of God.

A similarly effective influence is to be found in many texts familiar from prayer and worship. During daily morning prayer the account of human ‘good works’ (extended from Mishna Peah I: 1) is followed by several blessings which name the divine but also comparable works of God: ‘Praised be Thou, Lord, our God, King of the world, who makes the blind to see. Praised be Thou ... who clothes the naked. Praised be Thou... who frees the captives...’

Whoever prays psalm 145 three times a day – it appears in the liturgy that often every day – will be so formed by the teaching of this psalm that he too will ‘open his hand’ and may hope for a share of the life of the world to come.[19]

May we also describe the Sabbath celebration as imitation of

God? Ex. 20 : 11 and 31 : 17 might be called in evidence here. To be sure, God wrote about Himself; He rested, although there is no question of work as far as He is concerned;[20] and to that extent the Sabbath celebrated God as the Creator of all things rather than representing a human derivation of the divine completion and close of work. Just as, however, the Torah mentions diverse reasons for the Sabbath (cf. Ex. 20 : 11, together with Ex. 23 : 12 and Deut. 5 : 12–5), its celebration includes various motivational emphases, one of which is certainly that described thus by a Palestinian synagogue poet of the sixth century:

> Day of rest for the weary
> and repose for the exhausted,
> for then you are at peace from your work
> and rest from your labour,
> you bless it with your blessing
> and sanctify it with your sanctity,
> on it you rejoice at your works...[21]

Here I cannot go into the question whether in some human or specifically Jewish activities which the Haggadah ascribes to God, what is referred to is His exemplary teaching which Israel should learn and follow, or – at the same time – an 'imitatio hominis' or of Israel by God.[22]

I shall close this discussion of the explicit 'imitation-texts' with a haggadah which aptly illustrates the connection between imitatio dei and 'imitatio hominis' with reference to the question: Who takes the first step – God or man?: 'God is good to all and His compassion is over all that He has made (Ps. 145 : 9). R. Joshua ben Levi (interpreted thus): The Lord is good to all and His compassion is over all, for they are His works. R. Shmuel bar Nachman (interpreted thus): The Lord is good to all and His compassion is over all, for it is consonant with His nature to be merciful ("His works" understood as: ruling his elect). R. Joshua (interpreted thus): in the name of R. Levi: The Lord is good to all and He (also) bestows His mercy upon mankind. R. Abba said: If tomorrow there is a lean year and men show mercy to one another, then the Lord too, may He be praised, will also show His mercy to them. – In the days of R. Tanḥuma Israel was in need of a fast (on account of drought), so they approached him and said: "Master, appoint a fast!" He appointed a fast for one day, for two days, for a third day, yet no rain fell. Thereupon he mounted (the pulpit) and preached thus to them: "My children, be full of mercy one to the other and the Lord, may He be praised, will be merciful to you". And when they now gave help to the poor, they saw how a man passed money to his divorced wife; so they went to him (R. Tanḥuma) and said: "Such a person has passed money to his divorced wife". He had both of them brought before him and said to him: "Why have you passed money to your divorced wife?" He answered: "I saw that she was in great poverty, and I was overwhelmed with sympathy". Then R. Tanḥuma turned his face up to heaven and called out: "Lord of all worlds! This man, who is in no way responsible for this woman, saw her impoverished, and sympathy for her overwhelmed him – You, of whom it is written: The Lord is merciful and gracious (Ps. 103 : 8), and we (are) your children, the children of your friends, the children of Abraham, Isaac and Jacob, how much more should you be full of mercy towards us!" Thereupon the rain fell and the world recovered'.[23]

God allows Himself to be moved to pity when a human example, which indeed merely imitates His behaviour to mankind or to Israel (!), so to speak shows Him that (at least) one man is merciful 'gratis'. Fasting and beneficence produce nothing; only an action 'within the line of justice' can impel R. Tanḥuma's appeal and its answer.

Apart from the ethico-practical *imitation* of God as a superior human activity, there is also a *similarity* of Israel to God, which is in some measure preordained by God: a 'conformitas' which is less dynamic than static, and which has produced a rhetoric of polarity and reciprocity, an all-inclusive antithesis of God and Israel.

First impressions notwithstanding, these hymnlike 'circumstantial descriptions' may be classed among considerations of active ethical imitation. The ideas of Israel's likeness to God and comparability to God by reason of its 'incomparability' are associated with the rabbinic statements which hardly touch upon these topics, and give them a to some extent cosmic motivation which is sometimes latent though not explicit. To be sure, this is grounded upon scriptural reference, and therefore may be understood as a development in accordance with Scripture, yet it is hardly conceivable without any Greek or neo-Platonic influence. Even though they are to be found in the Midrash, antithetical statements find their proper *Sitz im Leben*, or existential context, in hymnic liturgical poetry, which developed rapidly from the fifth century, because they fit a genre which is intended less to teach and to threaten than to re-invoke the activity of God and the ancestors, and ask for salvation and redemption. The poet Yannai expresses the notion of similarity thus:

> Who is like you and who is like your people?
> Who is similar to you – but they are similar to you!
> You have chosen them for yourself, they have chosen you for themselves
> They for you and your for them
> Ordained for you and them alike
> The same names for you and them
> They are called by your name, the 'holiness of Israel'
> You are called by their name, 'Holy Israel'
> You say: I am your sanctifier and your sanctification
> You are my sanctified and my sanctification
> Worthy the sanctification of the Holy by the holy![24]

The similarity of Israel to the Lord produced and testified to by God himself is here skilfully demonstrated by means of an association of 'names'. It would not be inaccurate to see this correspondence of 'above' and 'below' as stemming from Greek sources, as their influence is evident above all in Philo of Alexandria. Here, too, the idea of likeness unto God (Gen. 1 : 26) is extended and further developed, without however becoming a ground for ethical imitation.[25] Correspondence and reciprocity provoke the rise of ideal qualifications such as the foregoing, in which the afflictions of time and human imperfection are overshadowed by the election of Israel, which may be understood both as deriving historically from Sinai, and cosmically from 'before the creation'. This preordained similarity is complementary to the active sanctification of God and the following of His ways – in other words, active imitatio requires a desire to correspond to God. Moreover, commissions and omissions in regard to the secondary image 'below' are important for the primary and model image 'above'.

An association of likeness, 'conformitas', with ethical imitation is to be expected. A work of the early Middle Ages had God address Moses (on whom He once again bestows His forgiveness) as follows:

Am I not the One whose sons you are,
and whose Father I am?
You are my brothers,
I am your Brother.
You my friends,
I your Friend.
You my loved ones,
I your loved One.
Have I allowed you to lack anything?
I ask from you nothing more
than what I found in Myself
– eleven qualitites;
these eleven you too should have,
namely these:
'Whoever walks in the ways of perfection, does right,
speaks the truth from his heart,
whoever does not calumniate with his tongue,
whoever does his neighbour no mischief
and does not slander his neighbours...,
who does that, will not waver'.[26]

Psalm 15, in other words, applied both to Israel and to God, grounded in the antithesis of Father and sons, Brother and brothers, Loved One and loved ones.

I shall now summarize the consequences for the 'classical' rabbinic period, as the constitutive phase of Judaism up to the present.

The mediation of the Absolute by means of indirect imitation of God in the form of human models is all but unknown. God 'Himself' is an anthropomorphically conceived ethical example without any conceptually abstract terminology. His middṓt serve to reveal those of his 'aspects' that are worthy of imitation or rather, imitable, so that man can experience and learn thus how he should behave humanely towards his neighbours. Nevertheless, specific activities are not allocated to each middṓt in such a way that individual middṓt would 'personify' specific ethical actions. The attributes of graciousness and mercy are prominent: the 'works of loving-kindness' issue from them.

Men, on the other hand, act as models only by virtue of certain specific qualitites, for instance Moses in the case of humility, Aaron of love of peace, or Hillel of patience. For all His transcendent incomparability, God is the One who reveals Himself in His Torah, His commandments and His 'ways'. To walk in these ways means imitatio dei towards one's fellow men and the whole creation (Ps. 145!). Hence the known works of gemilut ḥassadim are gradually joined by a psychologically refined conception which begins to deduce further divine attributes, such as forbearance with sinners, bearing with calumny, and so on.[27]

The anthropomorphism and anthropomorpathy of popular rabbinic exegesis and preaching, and the speculatively anthropomorphic literature of esoteric groups, came under the harsh criticism of Karaite and Islamic rationalism. Under their influence the idea of God had to be 'purified' from all forms of pietistic and popular anthropomorphism, and had to be appropriately reformulated in philosophical language.

R. Moshe ben Maimon (Maimonides, 1135–1204) was the most significant figure in the struggle within Judaism against anthropomorphism and any possible threat from positive attributes to the oneness and incorporeality of God. Like Philo, Maimonides made use of allegorical interpretation and excluded from his negative theology all positive statements about God – even 'greatness', 'graciousness' and 'omnipotence'. All attributes whatever ascribed to God are only effective attributes. Maimonides loses no opportunity of asserting: 'God possesses no ethical characteristics, but acts in a way to which our actions, which derive from ethical qualities, are similar'. And: 'The highest human virtue is to become like unto Him, in so far as man is capable of that: that is, we must make our behaviour like His, as the sages have indicated with the explanation of 'You should be holy': He is gracious, be gracious also; He is merciful, be merciful also. The purpose of all this is to show that the attributes ascribed to Him are those of His activity and do not signify that He possesses characteristics'.[28] Elsewhere, however, Maimonides also stresses knowledge more emphatically as the way to God.

The gulf between the expurgated notion of God of the philosophers and the naive 'model' of the simple and pious should not be overlooked.

Therefore Maimonides in his practice-oriented books with their dual impulsion – both talmudic and halachic *and* philosophical – was concerned to represent and hand on the traditional teaching of the active imitation of God, without any possible misinterpretations of God in the abovementioned sense. In Maimonides' work, and in the other medieval compendia of the 613 commandments and proscriptions, the commandment to imitate God is well to the fore. The commandments which are contextually close to it – dependence on Him, loving Him, fearing Him, hallowing His name, and so on – show clearly that here we have no exposition of systematic theology but several new attempts to do justice theologically and in terms of practice to the fulness of the reciprocal relationship between God and Israel. Hence the summons to imitate God was handed on from the twelfth century to the present day in the form of a commandment with an authentically biblical and rabbinic derivation.

But neo-Platonic elements of Judaism which continued more or less under the surface in the Middle Ages, together with the negative theology of Maimonidean origin in the sixteenth century, ensured an astonishing intensification and transformation of the notion of imitation.

The sixteenth-century Kabbalah, in the form of a short, very influential and still popular work, was no less effective than the abovementioned lapidary and pragmatic commandments. A few words of Jewish 'mysticism' must suffice to explain this.

The Divine has two aspects in the Kabbalah: first, the hidden and unattainable, the 'en sof', the Infinite, of which absolutely nothing can be predicated; even the Torah does not know this aspect of God which is free of all anthropomorphism (it is the paradoxical fulness of divine Nothingness); and second, the aspect of the open, accessible God, whose manifestation is the Torah. The Torah describes the process of divine becoming, divine inward life, for the truly percipient.

In this divine becoming there is a primal movement of the en sof outwards from itself into the form of manifestation. This is not creation, therefore, but emanations which are themselves divine in substance, describable in an extremely complex organism of ten metaphysical powers, the Sefiroth, stages or manifestations, instruments of the self-revealing God – a highly esoteric and speculative doctrine indeed, which however in the seventeenth century became a widely acknowledged system for the understanding of the life, fate and destination of an oppressed Israel. The interdependence of the divine and human realms is very great. Sin and Israel's suffering condition in the world reflect a fissure in the inward life of God. Every thought and action is of great significance; by their influence on the delicate relations within the

Sefiroth, they can increase the fissure and extend the exile of Israel or, positively, bring redemption closer by a life of sanctity. Hence greater significance is ascribed to imitatio dei than hitherto – in all active and passive areas of life.[29]

Against this background there appeared an unpretentious ethical treatise by one of the great Safed Kabbalists, R. Moshe Cordovero (1522-1570), with the unusual title, The Palm Tree of Deborah.[30]

Since man reflects God in his life and by living a life in accordance with God can introduce harmony into life and the associated powers of the divine Sefiroth, Cordovero tries to show the way in which each of the ten Sefiroth can be perfected by human thought and action in the light of the qualities revealed in each Sefirah.

Within the first, highest Sefirah, 'Crown', there are thirteen attributes (middṓt) of mercifulness, which it is given to man to imitate. These are not the thirteen known to us from Ex. 34 : 6 f (or the eleven of Ps. 15) but 'higher' attributes which Cordovero finds alluded to in Micah 7 : 18–20. The book begins thus:

'It becomes man to imitate his Creator and to resemble Him in image and likeness in accordance with the mystery of higher form. Similarity only in external appearance and not in deeds would betray form. Of him who approximates to form only physically, it is said: "A beautiful form and despicable actions". What profit would there be in resembling higher form in the likeness of members of the body without resembling the Creator in deeds? Hence it becomes man to cleave to the action of perfection, the thirteen middṓt of mercy, which are indicated in the following (Micah 7: 18–20):

'Who is a God like You,
who suffers sin
and remits the guilt of those
who remain from his inheritance?
He does not sustain his anger for ever,
for He loves mercy.
He will be merciful to us again,
trample our guilt under foot and cast
all our sins
into the depths of the ocean.
You will keep faith with Jacob, and

be bountiful to Abraham,
as You promised our forefathers in
ancient times'.

The first middah: 'Who is a God like thee?' shows, says Cordovero, that the Lord is a patient (ne 'elab) King who bears with insults in a way that goes beyond the bounds of human understanding. Every man is indeed nourished at all times by God's superabundance, and lives by virtue of divine power. Therefore no one sins against God unless divine power keeps him alive. God does not withdraw from the sinner, although He could allow him to perish at any time:

'God could say: "If you sin against me, then do that through your own power, not mine." He does not do it, and suffers the reproach. "Who is a God like you?" That is to say: You, the God of loving-kindness and mercy, are *God*, with the power to demand and requite, yet You are patient... Behold, that is behaviour which we should adopt: to be patient and to suffer abuse to the last degree, and yet not to deny the recipient our loving-kindness'.

This is the lowest stage. Cordovero closes each stage with advice on how to put it into actual practice. Even the well-known works of love, gemilut ḥassadim, obtain in the light of the Sefiroth teaching new significance for the restoration of the full, divinely-immanent harmony – works of compassion in God – the burial of the dead is among them.

Maimonides and Cordovero and many successors in popular ethical literature determine even for the present day the specifically Jewish version of the idea and realization of an imitation of God.

The question how Judaism has maintained the God–man antithesis in the imitation of God is something that I shall now try to answer. It would not be possible without different ways of mediation between God and man, whether by means of 'anthropomorphic' exemplary behaviour on the part of God, or His 'attributes', His 'ways' and 'names', and especially the Sefiroth of the Kabbalah. Their function of mediation between the transcendence and 'co-humanity' of God does not however amount to personification. There is no dissolution of the antithetical tension in a paradigmatic man and his imitation, as happens in Christianity and (though in a different way) in Islam.[31] Certainly we know certain paradigmatic individuals, such as the Zaddikim of Hassidism, whom one follows in the search for the living Torah, in order through them to cleave to God; these are in fact always fellow humans and contemporaries, who cannot be described as 'saints' in the conventional Christian sense. God Himself is the lasting paradigm for what man should do in regard to men – and to God: actual everyday fellow humanity. In this respect we should not forget that there are commandments of commission and omission whose content is not 'God's ways' but which are 'nothing' but his commandments.

The question I raised intitially of the power and relevance of the idea today is difficult to answer, especially for non-Jews. There are several reasons for this. Of course it seems as if traditional religious Judaism were continuing on its way undeterred by the events of the years 1933-45, but the effects on the entire Jewish people of the disasters of the last four decades are not yet predictable. In quite general terms, we can say only that the idea of an imitation of God occurs in discussion of socio-ethical problems in several currents of contemporary Judaism. The firm orientation to practice shows how attractive the idea is.

The answer is difficult for reasons of temporal history alone, but is even more so because of a problem of cultural history which affects the theme of imitation of God. The burial societies always held their annual celebration on the seventh day of Adar, according to tradition the day on which Moses died. In so doing they did not think of the imitation of God as such, even though there was a special significance for them in this choice of date. Traditional Judaism certainly did not theorize about the 'imitation of God' beyond the level of such allusions. The consideration of elements of Jewish thought which treat of the imitation of God began only in the present century, and is not yet complete. Its initial impulsion to no small degree arose from apologetical concern aroused by the general confrontation with Christianity. Therefore it took effect first of all in conceptions and structures which were far more strongly marked by Greek or Christian influence than derived from specifically Jewish criteria. I have already mentioned that Judaism knows no abstract category which would be equivalent to the Latin imitatio dei. Yet imitation of God may be described as obvious and important for Judaism. Its ramifications are to be found in many related ideas which connot easily be subsumed under western notions and categories. Within Judaism they are still characterized in biblical terms: for instance, serving Him, cleaving to Him, walking in the ways of God, and so on. These, and others, belong to the Jewish context of imitation. Moreover the effects of Cordovero's teaching on imitation by way of ethical literature with a kabbalist emphasis right up to our own times, and their possible contemporary significance, have not been analyzed. Research into independent structures of Jewish teaching and activity in regard to the imitation of God has yet to be carried out.

What are the consequences of what A.J. Heschel formulated thus: God's desire for man is not 'to obey what He wills but to *do* what He is'? [32]

## Notes

1 The text of Is. 64 : 4 is difficult; accordingly this translation is one of many possibilities.
Literature on the topic:
I. Abraham, 'The Imitation of God', in: Studies in Pharisaism and the Gospels II (New York, second edition, 1967), pp. 138–82; F. Böhl, 'Das rabbinische Verständnis des Handelns in der Nachahmung Gottes', Zs. für Missionswissenschaft und Religionswissenschaft, 58 (1974), pp. 134–41; M. Buber, Nachahmung Gottes, Werke Vol. II (Munich, 1964), (ET: 'Imitatio Dei', in: Israel and the World, New York, 1948, pp. 66–84); A. Funkenstein, 'Imitatio Dei umussag haṣimṣum bemishnat ḤaBaD' (Hebrew), in: R. Mahler Jubilee Volume (Tel Aviv, 1974), pp. 83–8; I. Heinemann, 'Das Ideal der Heiligkeit im hellenistischen und rabbinischen Judentum', in: Jeschurun, 8 (1921), pp. 99–120; H. Kosmala, 'Nachfolge und Nachahmung Gottes' II: 'Im jüdischen Denken', in: Annual of the Swedish Theological Institute, 3 (1964), pp. 65–110; A. Marmorstein, Die Nachahmung Gottes (Imitatio Dei) in der Agada. Jüdische Studien Dr. J. Wohlgemuth gewidmet... (Frankfurt am Main, 1928), pp. 144–59; ET in The A.M. Memorial Volume. Studies in Jewish Theology. Eds. J. Rabbinowitz & M.S. Lew (London, 1950; Farnborough, [2]1970), pp. 106–21; H.J. (Leon) Roth, Hahiddamut la'el ureʿajon haqedusha. Religion and Human Values. Selected Essays, ed. Z. Adar (Hebrew) (Jerusalem, 1973), pp. 20–30.

2 Pinkas Hakehillot, Encyclopaedia of Jewish Communities from their Foundation till after the Holocaust. Germany Bavaria (Hebrew) (Jerusalem, 1972), cf. Regensburg, p. 188.

3 The main relevant terms are: Meḥaqe, imitating (Hapax?) in a parable of Abba Shaul, Sifra Qedoshim, beginning. In Midrash and piyyut there is often the root dmh. The term occasionally used nowadays, hiddamut, similarity, making like unto, is of medieval origin. In Hebrew the biblical terminology 'walking in his way', 'cleaving to him' (or his qualities) and so on is used. In other languages: 'imitatio dei' and its equivalents.

4 H. Kosmala, op. cit., p. 96. The first part of the study: in Greek thought, in ASTI 2 (1963), pp. 38–85. Kosmala derives his conclusions wholly from Greek or Christian thought and fits the Jewish material to his theory.

[5] See, e.g., H. Loewe in C.G. Montefiore & H. Loewe, A Rabbinic Anthology (New York, ²1974), pp. 43 ff.

[6] Thus L. Roth, op. cit., p. 22.

[7] Sifra Qedoshim on Lev. 19 : 2: '"You shall be holy!" – You shall be set apart, you shall be holy because I am holy, the Lord, your God. The meaning is if you make yourselves holy, I look upon it as though you made me holy, and if you do not make yourselves holy, I look upon it as though you had not made me holy. Does that mean if you make me holy, then I am holy, and if you do not then I am not made holy? Rather "because I am holy". I am in my holiness, whether you make me holy or not!'

[8] See the fourth rule in the introduction of the Sefer hamiṣwot, ed. J. Kafiḥ (Jerusalem, 1971), pp. 18 ff: '... Lev. 19 : 2 and 11 : 44 are summons to fulfil the whole Torah, as though he (God) had said: Be holy in doing that which I command you to do, and keep yourself from what I warned you against'.

[9] Cf. Meqhilta deRabbi Yish'mael, beshallaḥ 3, ed. Horovitz-Rabin, p. 127; Mequilta de Rabbi Shimᶜon b. Yoḥai, beshallaḥ 15, ed. Epstein-Melamed, p. 79; yPea 1 : 1–15b; bShab, 133b; Yalqut Ex. 15 : 2 par. 244; 244; Soferim 3 : 13; anonymous: Sifre Deut. on 11 : 22 par. 49; R. Ḥama b. Ḥanina: bSota 14a.

[10] Fragmentary Targum (TJ II) on Gen. 35 : 9. Targum PsJonathan (TJ I) on Deut. 34 : 6; cf. TPsJ on Ex. 18 : 20.

[11] bSota 14a.

[12] To address God in the second person is typical of the berakḥa formula which appears at the beginning and/or end of the prescribed prayers. Their eulogies are usually in the present tense. Cf. the second benediction of the tephillah (Prayer of the Eighteen Benedictions): 'You sustain the living with loving-kindness; you quicken the dead with great mercy. You support the falling and heal the sick, loosen the bound and keep faith with them who sleep in the dust. Who is like You, Master of might, and who can be compared to You, O King, Author of death and of life. Who causes salvation to sprout? You are faithful to quicken the dead. You are praised, O Lord, who quickens the dead!' In the daily grace after meals: '... and day after day He loved us and loves us and will love us, helped us and continues to help us, with love, with loving-kindness, with tenderness... And may love, life, salvation and good of all kinds never be lacking in us'.

[13] Sifre Deut. on 11 : 22 par. 49, ed. Finkelstein, p. 114. 'God is called X – You are X'. Here a usage is developing which would support R. Moshe b. Maimon in the twelfth century when he rejected any metaphysical divine attribute and understood his titles only as 'effective modes' experienced by human beings.

[14] Sifre Deut., ibid.

[15] E.g., Jacob Joseph of Polnoy; see G. Nig'al, Torot baᶜal hatoldot Dershot R. Jaaqob Josef... (Jerusalem, 1974), pp. 95 ff.

[16] L. Roth, p. 25, finds together with Aḥad haAm an important Jewish aspect here. It is not imitation per se but the selective restriction that would count. It is possible that here we have a not unimportant distinction from the Christian idea of imitatio which, as imitatio Christi, does not require that Christ should be imitated in all regards.

[17] Genesis Rabba 49 : 8, ed. Theodor-Albeck, p. 508.

[18] bSukka, 30a.

[19] Cf. H. Loewe, introduction, in: A Rabbinic Anthology, eds., C.G. Montefiore & H. Loewe (New York, ²1974), p. lxxxviii.

[20] MekhY on Ex. 20 : 11, Lorovitz-Rabin, p. 230.

[21] Piyyute Yannai, ed. M. Zulay (Berlin & Jerusalem, 1938), Qeroba 44 on Ex. 16 : 28, pp. 98f. On the discussion of the motivation of the Sabbath celebration, see L. Jacobs, Faith (London, 1968), p. 167.

[22] Cf. in this regard H. Kosmala, II, p. 110, n. 163.

[23] GenR, 33 : 3, ed. Theodor-Albeck, pp. 304ff; cf. LevR, 34 : 14, ed. Margylies, pp. 806–9.

[24] Piyyute Yannai, ed. Zulay, Qeroba 70 on Lev. 19 : 2, p. 159.

[25] On the similarities and contrasts in Philo between 'above' and 'below', kosmos noetos and kosmos aisthetos, of which Israel is the cosmological expression, see B.L. Mack, 'Imitatio Mosis: Patterns of Cosmology and Soteriology in the Hellenistic Synagogue', in: Studia Philonica 1 (1972), pp. 27–55. Mack shows that Philo tries to unite the disparate themes and tendencies of Israel's 'cosmic way' toward a 'more continuous anthropological paradigm', and sees Moses as the unique hero-representative, so that there has to be an 'imitatio Mosis'.

[26] Seder Eliyahu Rabba, ed. Friedmann, ch. 14, p. 65.

[27] SER, ch. 24 end, p. 135; MidrPss 86 : 1, ed. Buber, p. 372.

[28] More Nebuqhim I, 54; cf. Mishne Torah, Hilkhot Deʿot 1 : 6f.

[29] A comprehensive and at the same time practical overall study of the Kaballah is available in G. Scholem, Kabbalah (in English) (Jerusalem, 1974); see also, ib., On the Kabbalah and its Symbolism (New York, 1965); On Moshe Cordovera see pp. 401–4 and further, in ibid.

[30] 'Tomer Debora', various editions. English translation with introduction by L. Jacobs (ed.), Rabbi Moses Cordovera, The Palm Tree of Deborah (London, 1960).

[31] On the imitation of the Prophet, see A. Schimmel, 'The Prophet Muhammad as a Centre of Muslim Life and Thought', in: A. Schimmel & A. Falaturi, We Believe in One God: The Experience of God in Christianity and Islam (London & New York, 1979), pp. 35–61, esp. 37–48.

[32] A.J. Heschel, God in Search of Man. A Philosophy of Judaism (New York, $^{2}$1970), p. 290.

# From Jesus the 'Prophet' to Jesus the 'Son'

*Franz Mussner*

Ecumenical dialogue between representatives of the three monotheistic world religions should not ignore whatever is proper to each, which specific content also constitutes their essential difference one from another. That which is proper to Christianity is contained explicitly in Christology. Yet those doctrines of faith and aspects of faith proper to each religion often have much in common, which can be taken into consideration if all the participants in the discussion are willing. The common element in Christology is without doubt that of the 'prophet'. For the concept of the 'prophet' is also found in Judaism, in its Holy Scripture, the 'Old Testament'; likewise it forms one of the central tenets of Islamic faith. Even though the early Church did not confine itself to a 'prophetic Christology', Jesus of Nazareth was in fact experienced and proclaimed as a 'prophet', as can be seen from the Gospels. It is frequently overlooked, however, even in Christian theology, that there is a genetic connection between the Christological predicate 'Son' and the prophetic predicate used to describe Jesus of Nazareth.

Jesus came from Nazareth in Galilee. After he had begun to appear publicly in Israel, he returned one day, as Mark tells us, 'to his own country. And on the sabbath he began to teach in the synagogue; and many who heard him were astonished, saying: "Where did this man get all this? What is the wisdom given to him? What mighty works are wrought by his hands! Is not this the carpenter, the son of Mary and brother of James and Joses and Judas and Simon, and are not his sisters here with us?" And they took offence at him. And Jesus said to them, "A prophet is not without honour, except in his own country, and among his own kin, and in his own house".' (Mk. 6 : 1–4).

From this account we learn that Jesus came from Nazareth, that he was a 'carpenter' by trade, and that his family also lived in Nazareth. When rejected by his own people after appearing in public, Jesus comments that 'a prophet is not without honour, except in his own country, among his own kind, and in his own house'. Thus Jesus of Nazareth makes an explicit claim to be considered as something akin to a 'prophet'. The opinions of the people of Israel as to who this man from Nazareth really was would seem to have followed the same direction, as is borne out by two further accounts in Mark. In 6 : 14f Mark states the following: 'King Herod heard of it; for Jesus' name had become known. Some said, "John the baptizer has been raised from the dead; that is why these powers are at work in him". But others said, "It is Elijah". And others said, "It is a prophet, like one of the prophets of old".'

According to Mk. 8 : 27f, Jesus personally asked his disciples one day: 'Who do men say that I am?' And they told him, 'John the Baptist; and others say Elijah; and others one of the prophets.' On the raising of the young man of Naim, Luke comments: 'Fear seized them all; and they glorified God, saying, "A great prophet has arisen among us!" and "God has visited his people!" ' (Lk. 7: 16). The two disciples who walk to Emmaus on Easter Sunday summarize the experience of Jesus as follows: 'Concerning Jesus of Nazareth, who was a prophet mighty in deed and word before God and all the people' (Lk. 24 : 19). According to Jn. 6 : 14, those present at the miracle of the loaves and fishes exclaimed that 'this is indeed the prophet who is to come into the world!' And the same applies to those who witnessed Jesus preach, as in Jn. 7 : 40: 'This is really the prophet'. When the blind man whose sight Jesus restored is asked 'What do you say about him, since he has opened your eyes?' he answers: 'He is a prophet' (Jn. 9 : 17). According to Lk. 13 : 33, Jesus states that 'It cannot be that a prophet should perish away from Jerusalem'. G. Friedrich comments on this: 'As in Mk. 6 : 4, Jesus is not describing himself, but rather referring to a generally accepted opinion. But the fact that he not only adopts this opinion but also sets about fulfilling it means that he sees himself as included in the ranks of the prophets'.[1] According to Mt. 21 : 10f, when Jesus entered Jerusalem 'all the city was stirred, saying: ,,Who is this?" And the crowds said, "This is the prophet Jesus from Nazareth of Galilee".' And in Mt. 21 : 46, the evangelist comments: 'But when they tried to arrest him, they feared the multitude, because they held him to be a prophet'.

To sum up, it can be seen[2] that although Jesus of Nazareth did not expressly describe himself as a prophet, the people who witnessed his miracles did regard him as one. At various points in the New Testament, Jesus is clearly seen as the promised *prophet of the last days*, following Deut. 18 : 15[2a]. G. Friedrich finally reaches the conclusion 'that Jesus never explicitly refers to himself as a prophet of the last days, but that this cannot be seen as proof that he did not consider himself to be a prophet; rather, it corresponds to his other pronouncements concerning the mystery of the Messiah. But he spoke and acted like a prophet'.[3] Almost all Jesus' actions can be related to the prophetic element. Jesus' calling, his awareness of his mission, his criticism of the Torah and ritual, his directives concerning his successors (at least to a certain extent), his declarations of doom (threatening words and lamentations), his symbolic actions and miraculous deeds, his spiritual gifts and finally his violent death – to name but the most important – all belong to the prophetic tradition.[4]

For this reason, it is understandable that at first, especially in the early Judaeo-Christian Church in Palestine, prophetic Christology should have predominated. Was this subsequently suppressed by the Christology of the Son? For example, under the influence of Hellenism, when the Christian mission had spread beyond the boundaries of the Holy Land and in the defensive tendencies which manifested themselves early on in Judaeo-Christianity, which resulted in Jesus being seen as nothing more than a prophet (cf. pseudo-Clementines)?[5] The question is whether a prophetic Christology could naturally grow into a Christology of the Son. Cullman is of the opinion that the presentation of Jesus in the New Testament as a 'prophet' is only adduced as a popular opinion which was probably 'widespread especially in Galilee'.[6] F. Hahn concedes that 'at an early stage in tradition Jesus' person and deeds were described in terms of the eschatological prophet', but that this was 'obscured and obliterated by later Christological pronouncements' and that 'certain idiosyncracies of this traditional Christology could still be discerned'.[7] I, too, shared this opinion for a long time until I came across U. Mauser's book Gottesbild und Menschwerdung.[8] This work not only helped me to see the Christology of the prophet in a new light, but also to see it as a decisive preparatory stage towards a Christology of the Son; and furthermore to comprehend not only the origins of the latter, but its significance. It must strike anyone who studies the Gospel that the old Christology of the prophet dating from the earliest days of the Church was not suppressed by the Gospel compilers. Indeed, the Gospels are our main source of knowledge about it. But this raises the question why the evangelists did not suppress it, instead of linking it with the Christology of the Son so that the latter embraced the former, thereby interpreting and surpassing it. How does Mauser see this?

Mauser's starting point is an article by the Old Testament theologian W. Zimmerli, 'Promise and Fulfilment' (Verheißung und Erfüllung),[9] in which Zimmerli establishes two facts (I am quoting Mauser's paraphrase of his argument): 'First, it can be proved that the apparent fulfilment of a concrete promise in the Old Testament weakens the sense of finality and in turn becomes the basis for a new promise far exceeding the fulfilment apparently already achieved'; on the other hand 'that Israel's expectations are not essentially directed towards any particular end apart from the coming of God'.[10] Zimmerli quotes the words of the prophet Amos (4 : 12): 'Prepare to meet your God, O Israel!' He states that 'the focus of all promises is the coming of the Lord himself'.[11] Mauser then tentatively links this promise with its fulfilment in Jesus Christ: 'The coming of God in the New Testament is in fact his coming into the history of a human being; this is the unique aspect of the New Testament message, that God carries out his entire task through a single human destiny'.[12] This leads Mauser to ask 'whether it is possible, indeed whether it is demanded by the nature of the Old Testament promise, to find proof in the Old Testament for the coming of God in human form?'[13] Whereas for Bultmann the human existence bound up with the name 'Jesus of Nazareth' is of significance only in so far as it 'is a prerequisite for the coming of the kerygma' (Mauser),[14] Mauser is concerned with the eschatological coming of Yahweh, as foretold by the prophets, precisely in the human existence of Jesus, in his life before Easter right up to his violent death and resurrection. 'Jesus' human existence, as the basis of the Christian kerygma, is the Word of God. This human existence proves itself to be the point of convergence of several lines of argument raised by both the Old and New Testament'. This leads one to ask in turn: '... whether this point of convergence could not form the starting point for a rethinking of the problem of the relationship between the Old and the New Testament. With respect to the Old Testament the question is as follows: If the Old Testament is to be understood as a promise, waiting in expectation of the coming of God in concrete terms as his coming in the form of a human existence, then we must ask ourselves if the image of God in the Old Testament has any characteristics which testify to God's inclination to assume human form. This divine image would have to correspond to a human image according to which human existence is destined to fulfil itself as the Word of God embodied in human history. With respect to the New Testament, we must ask whether the history which Christian theology has for centuries described as the incarnation of God can be seen as a genuine human history so that it corresponds to the basic structures of the Old Testament image of God and man'.[15]

In order to make his approach clear to the reader, Mauser refers to the so-called anthropomorphisms of the Old Testament, which he sees as 'indications of a God who is not remote from humanity and who participates in the history of mankind by assuming human characteristics. This corresponds simultaneously to the image of man contained in the Old Testament which... in a certain sense is theomorphic, because, according to the history of creation, man is 'the image and likeness' of God. Alluding to a formulation of the hymn to Christ in the Letter to the Philippians, Mauser states that 'the God of the Old Testament ἐν μορφῇ ἀνθρώπου is the proclamation of Deus incarnatus. And the image of man in the Old Testament who to a certain extent experiences his life ἐν μορφῇ θεοῦ is the precursor of Jesus-made-man who corresponds to the Christian creed of vere Deus'.[16] Mauser thus establishes his theme. He pursues it in three ways through that part of his book devoted to the Old Testament. First, he examines further the theological meaning of 'anthropomorphisms', and then interprets the fate of the prophets Hosea and Jeremiah by means of their texts so that through their fate the fate of Yahweh himself may be discerned in his sorrowful and painful dialogue with the people of Israel. Hence the prophets of the Old Covenant are not seen merely as critics of the established order in Israel and as harbingers of salvation and disaster; rather, they are seen as Yahweh's representatives. 'The God of Israel is a God full of pathos, and prophecy is the inspired communication of the divine pathos to the consciousness of the prophet', [17] as Mauser states in connection with the book The Prophet by the Jewish scholar Abraham J. Heschel.[17a]

With respect to the anthropomorphisms, Mauser remarks that

'Yahweh's anthropomorphisms have a corresponding relationship to the creation of man in God's image and are mutually explicable'.[18] Mauser quotes J. Hempel: 'For mankind, to be God's image... means to be his vizier'.[19] The Old Testament anthropomorphisms 'not only did not constitute a temporally determined naivety...', on the contrary they contain 'conscious theology' (Mauser).[20] Mauser goes on to refer to the book by the Old Testament theologian, H. Wheeler Robinson, The Cross of Hosea (1949) in which Robinson interprets the prophet Hosea, especially with regard to the first three chapters about the prophet's marriage, 'in a way which opened up a totally new dimension to the problem of anthropomorphism'.[21] The story of the prophet's marriage serves as 'a human illustration of a divine truth'. 'To begin with this has a bearing on the concept of revelation. So long as revelation is seen as the communication of truth, the process of revelation is still conceived in mechanical terms. Thus man, who receives the revelation, is seen as a mere scribe taking down a decree. The Book of Hosea however permits the opinion that this mechanical kind of conception does not correspond to the true process of revelation. For in Hosea – Mauser cites Robinson verbatim – 'we see that the revelation is made in and through human experience, in which experience the truth to be revealed is first created'. From this it follows 'that human experience is capable of representing the divine... revelation is made through the unity of fellowship between God and man and is born of their intercourse'. Quite simply, this means that even in the Old Testament revelation is fundamentally linked to incarnation, in the sense that the mediator of revelation (the prophet) through his own existence participates in the revelation; indeed that his own life is the source of the revelation and the means by which it is made known'.[22] With respect to anthropomorphisms, it follows that the anthropomorphisms of the Old Testament are in no sense 'mere gestures towards human weakness without expressive images for the truth of the living God'. On the contrary, God's caring and love are expressed not only in human speech, but are reflected representatively in the living experience and fate of the prophet. Hosea's love and caring are 'not only symbols of God's attitude to the world; they are also the real concrete equivalents of God's equally real love and caring. But any serious discussion of God's real love and caring clearly invalidates the dogma of God's impassibility'.[23] 'Anthropomorphism' in this sense is therefore the 'proclamation of God's incarnation'[24] ... And the prophet 'is the person who not only knows God's pathos so that he can transmit it, but experiences it in and for itself in such a way that it affects his whole being'.[25] Thus the central mystery of prophecy can be defined as 'sympathy with the divine pathos'.[26] 'And if there is a divine pathos, then there must also be a prophetic pathos stemming from and inspired by the divine pathos of which it is like a mirror reflection. Hence the prophet is not merely the announcer of God's decisions and directives; first and foremost he represents God's own position in the history of the world he created'.[27] Furthermore, the prophet differs from his contemporaries in that 'he knows what time it is and proclaims it as the time of God'.[28] The core of the prophetic existence is 'his participation in God's relationship with mankind in history, which is determined by the concrete hour of God'.[29] In the prophet God 'assumes human form', through him he appears ἐν μορφῇ ἀνθρώπου, which of course does not mean that the divine nature is 'fused' with human nature, or that God is 'incorporated' into the prophet.

By this means Mauser introduces an important aspect of the discussion. He pursues his thesis with reference to the prophets Hosea and Jeremiah. Hosea is able to 'act symbolically because he himself has already become a symbol of God'.[30] 'Yahweh's charge does not merely make of the prophet a messenger repeating received knowledge. Rather the word of God creates a human life which in human terms shares God's history'.[31] The anthropomorphic language of the Old Testament 'aims to reveal a God who assumes human qualities to such an extent that he can be represented by an actual human being'.[32] The prophet 'adopts the position of God towards the people in history, and he shares God's destiny, as experienced by Yahweh at the actual time of his action. Thus he is not only God's spokesman, but Yahweh's representative and image'.[33] Thus 'God's incarnation is prepared in the evidence of Israel's faith'.[34]

The New Testament accords completely with this, for it describes 'the work of God in the work of Jesus of Nazareth, in his words and in his deeds...'.[35] The New Testament identifies precisely 'the event of a human existence (namely that of Jesus of Nazareth) in God's words and deeds... For this reason it speaks of God much more openly and emphatically in the form of human language and action, human will and resolution, than is ever the case in the Old Testament. The anthropomorphic treatment of God in the Old Testament is taken to such an extreme in the New Testament that the latter can only be understood as its insuperable culmination'.[36]

Anyone who accepts the above will also be able to agree with my thesis that the so-called prophetic Christology of the Gospel is not merely a 'minor Christological issue' of little consequence. On the contrary, by its very nature it leads logically in the continued Christological reflections of the early Church to the Christology of the Son. What did the circle of disciples in fact experience through seeing Jesus of Nazareth? I should like to answer: *A perfect unity of action between Jesus and Yahweh, an unprecedented existential 'imitatio Dei', on the part of Jesus.* In order to give linguistic expression to this experience in the reflections following Easter the predicate of the Son gradually established itself, as it were involuntarily. For the ancient oriental approach, the sonship of the first-born manifests itself in exact imitation of the father! If we compare the material for a messianic Christology with that for a prophetic Christology in the synoptic tradition, the latter far outweighs the former, as has been demonstrated by the researches of Fr. Schnieder. As I already emphasized above, almost all Jesus' deeds can be categorized within a 'prophetic Christology'. 'A great prophet has arisen among us, and God has visited his people!' (Lk. 7 : 16); 'a prophet mighty in deed and word' (24 : 19): this is the kind of impression Jesus made on people. Even in the Gospel of John,[37] with its profoundly reflected Christology of the Son, the Christological model of the prophet still plays an important rôle.[38]

In conclusion I should like to state that the Christology of the Son found in the New Testament in no way stems solely from the original prophetic Christology. For 'Son' is not merely a substitute for 'prophet'. To the experience of Jesus as prophet was added the experience of a μεῖζον and πλεῖον in Jesus which transcended the prophetic model. But I shall not pursue this point further here.[39] My concern in this article is to show that the Christological model of the Son may be elucidated to a large extent (if not completely) by recourse to the prophetic model, thereby removing much of the 'scandalous' character of New Testament-Christian Christology of the Son as interpreted by the doctrines of the monotheistic religions. The linguistic model for the 'Christology of the Son' was provided by the Old Testament and Judaism, especially by their philosophy. The prophet's destiny is to manifest God's 'pathos'; through his words and deeds he enters into a unity of action with the μόνος θεός. Seen in these terms, the New Testament-Christian Christology of the Son does not constitute the paganization and 'acute Hellenization' of strict monotheism, as is claimed by Judaism and Islam; rather, *it represents the doctrine of the self-expression and self-alienation of the* μόνος θεός *in the world*. Like Judaism and Islam, the Church has at all times maintained a strict monotheism, though it has always proclaimed Jesus of Nazareth as 'the Son of God', and continues to do so today. The objection to the Christology of the Son raised by Judaism and Islam will persist in the future, but the 'prophetical model' can provide common ground for discussion.

## Notes

[1] Theologisches Wörterbuch zum Neuen Testament, VI, p. 843.

[2] See also G. Friedrich in: ThNb VI, 847–9; R. Schnackenburg, 'Die Erwartung des 'Propheten' nach dem Neuen Testament und den Qumran-Texten', in: Stud. Evang. (TU 73) (Berlin, 1959), pp. 622–39; E. Boismard, 'Jésus le Prophet par excellence, d'après Jean 10, 24–39', in: J. Gnilka (ed.), Neues Testament und Kirche (Festschrift für R. Schnackenburg) (Freiburg, 1974), pp. 160–71.

[2a] See also Jn. 6 : 14; 7 : 40; Acts 3 : 22 (in a speech by Peter); 7 : 37 (in the words of St. Stephen).

[3] G. Friedrich, op. cit., p. 849.

[4] To the latter compare O.H. Steck, Israel und das gewaltsame Geschick der Propheten (Neukirchen, 1967). And in general see F. Schnider, Jesus, der Prophet (Orbis Biblicus et Orientalis) (Fribourg & Göttingen, 1973).

[5] See Schnider, op. cit., pp. 241–55; H.J. Schnoeps, Theologie und Geschichte des Judenchristentums (Tübingen, 1949), pp. 71–118.

[6] Christologie des Neuen Testaments (Tübingen, 1966), pp. 34 f.

[7] Christologische Hoheitstitel (Göttingen, [3]1966), p. 351.

[8] Eine Untersuchung zur Einheit des Alten und des Neuen Testaments (Tübingen, 1971).

[9] Ev Th 12 (1952/3) 34–59, reprinted in: C. Westermann (ed.), Probleme alttestamentlicher Hermeneutik (Munich, 1960), pp. 69–101 (from which I quote).

[10] Mauser, Gottesbild und Menschwerdung, pp. 4f.

[11] Op. cit., p. 90.

[12] Ibid., p. 7.

[13] Ibid., p. 8.

[14] Ibid., p. 15.

[15] Ibid., pp. 16f.

[16] Ibid., p. 17.

[17] Ibid., p. 41.

[17a] Published in 1936; enlarged American edition The Prophets (New York, 1962).

[18] Mauser, op. cit., p. 38.

[19] Das Ethos des Alten Testaments (Berlin, [2]1964), p. 201.

[20] Op. cit., p. 39.

[21] Ibid., p. 39.
[22] Ibid., p. 40.
[23] Ibid.
[24] Op. cit., p. 41.
[25] Ibid., p. 42.
[26] Ibid.
[27] Ibid., p. 43.
[28] Ibid., p. 42.
[29] Ibid.
[30] Ibid., p. 74.
[31] Ibid., p. 76.
[32] Ibid.
[33] Ibid., pp. 115 f.
[34] Ibid., p. 116.
[35] Ibid., p. 117.
[36] Ibid., In this context see also P. Kuhn, Gottes Selbsterniedrigung in der Theologie der Rabbinen (Stud. zum A und NT, 17) (Munich, 1968). Drawing on a wide range of textual material, Kuhn points to the rôle played by the idea of God's pathos in rabbinic thought; he structures his chosen texts as follows: 1. God renounces his glory; 2. God in the service of mankind; 3. God offers Himself to mankind; 4. God descends from heaven to earth; 5. God limits Himself to a single sphere in the world. See also Kuhn's (as yet unpublished) theological dissertation Gottes Trauer und Klage in der rabbinischen Überlieferung (Regensburg, 1974); also J.Scharbert, Der Schmerz im Alten Testament (BBB 8) (Bonn, 1955), pp. 216–225 (Der Schmerz Yahwehs); K. Kotamori, Theology of the Suffering of God (London, 1970).
[37] See Jn. 4 : 19; 9 : 17; 1 : 21, 25; 6 : 14; 7 : 40, 52; 8 : 52f,
[38] See also Schnider, Jesus, der Prophet, pp. 191–230; R. Schnackenburg, Die Erwartung des 'Propheten' nach dem Neuen Testament und den Qumran-Texten, in: Stud. Ev. (TU 73) (Berlin, 1959), pp. 622–39.
[39] See also F. Mussner, 'Ursprünge und Entfaltung der neutestamentlichen Sohneschristologie. Versuch einer Rekonstruktion', in: L. Scheffczyk (ed.), Grundfragen der Christologie (Freiburg, 1975), pp. 77–113.

# Hope in the Islamic Understanding of Faith[1]

*Erwin Gräf*

The standard term in the Koran for 'to believe' is āmana, both in the Meccan and in the Medinan sections; it occurs very often. The Handwörterbuch des Islam (HWI) says in this respect:[2] 'The basic concept of the root ᵓmn is "peace of heart" and "security from fear"... But the fourth form can also mean "to render unafraid" or "to place one's trust in something or in someone"... There could also be some trace of the Syrian mehaimen (believing) and haimanūṯā (belief).

īmān means belief, muᵓmin believer. Belief is the profession of monotheism, as preached by Muḥammad, and of the Last Judgment. The relation to works has not been elucidated as yet, and there is still no speculation whether faith can wax and wane.

The Koran has two expressions for 'to hope': amal (only twice) and raga (more often, in both the Meccan and the Medinan sections (more numerous in the latter case). With two exceptions, the relevant verses refer to eschatology, to the judgment of the individual, and not therefore to the fate of the Islamic community (umma), its extension, its victories, the final Islamization of the world and so on.[3]

A few quotations may serve to illustrate the significance of the subject-matter. For instance, 18 : 110: 'Say [i.e., Muḥammad]: "I am but a mortal like yourselves. It is revealed to me that your Lord is one God. Let him that hopes to meet his Lord do what is right and worship none besides Him'. The commentator Baiḍāwī adds: '... him that hopes for a favourable encounter with Him or fears a bad encounter'. This alternative is missing from most Suras. It would appear that a meeting with God is of positive value in itself – for instance the contemplation of God. Only at a later date was the possibility of a meeting with the God of retribution included. 29 : 5–4: 'He that hopes to meet his Lord must know that Allah's appointed hour is sure to come'. In other words, God's recompense, or a meeting with Him, or the end, namely death, resurrection, judgment, punishment.[4] 33 : 21: '... those who look to Allah and the Last Day'; that is, God's recompense or a meeting with Him or the blessedness of the other world or the days of Allah (which by exception would refer to this world, and shows that the exegetes did not know exactly what certain expressions signified), and especially the Last Judgment. It is also said that rağā can mean hope as well as fear (as later in the edifying literature). 25 : 21–3: 'Those who do not hope to meet Us ask...'; that is, on account of their lack of faith in the resurrection or because they did not fear to meet Us in evil... 2 : 218–215: 'Those that have embraced the faith and those that have fled their land and fought for the cause of Allah, may hope for Allah's mercy. Allah is forgiving and merciful'. Similarly 17 : 57–59: 'Those [i.e., the idols] to whom they pray, themselves seek to approach their Lord, vying with each other to be near Him. They crave for His mercy and fear His punishment; for your Lord's punishment is terrible indeed'. Here, for once, reward and punishment are mentioned expressly.

In order to interpret the verse correctly, it is important to remember that what we have here is first and foremost a missionary sermon, used only subsequently as a community sermon and above all liturgically, in the setting both of community worship and of personal piety – partly for meditation. Here we must remember that Islam gave rise to an umma, a form of theocratic community, which also had to fulfil all state functions but had no formal teaching authority. Compare the following citations: Koran 3 : 103–4/99–100: 'Thus Allah makes plain to you His revelations, so that you may be rightly guided. Let there become of you a nation that shall speak for righteousness, enjoin justice, and forbid evil...' (3 : 110–6) and Rom. 13 : 1: 'Let every person be subject to the governing authorities. For there is no authority except from God, and those that exist have been instituted by God...' But there is no Church[5] in Islam and therefore no official, authorized cure of souls. That has been extremely important for the inner development of Islam. For that reason, certain emotional possibilities wholly recommended by the Koran are despised and generally obscured. Islam is restricted to pure orthodox doctrine in dogmatic theology (kalām), and to right behaviour as prescribed by the revealed Law (Šarīʿa).

The so-called creed of Abū Ḥanifa (699–767), the oldest orthodox profession of faith,[6] states: 1. We consider no one to be an unbeliever because of sin, nor do we deny such a one faith (as against the Harigites). – 2. We summon you to do what is good and forbid what is evil. – 3. What concerns you could not have failed you, and what you are lacking could not have affected you [predestination]. – 4. We deny non of the companions of God's Ambassador; we follow none of them exclusively. – 5. We leave aside the question of ᶜUṯmān and ᶜAlī Allah, Who knows mysteries and hidden things. – 6. Understanding in matters of religion is better than understanding in matters of knowledge and law. – 7. Difference of opinion in the community is a sign of Divine mercifulness. – 8. Whoever believes everything that he is bound to believe, but says: 'I do not know whether Moses and Jesus... belong among the messengers of God or not', is an unbeliever. – 9. Who says: 'I do not know if Allah is in Heaven or on earth', is an unbeliever'. – 10. Who says: 'I do not acknowledge punishment in the grave', belongs to the sect of the Ǧahmites,[7] which is bound for perdition.

Serious systematic theologians know that man cannot recognize all the characteristics of God, but only those which are most advantageous (aṣlaḥ) to him.[8]

Ethics is restricted to five 'pillars': the šahāda or testimony: 'There is no God but Allah, and Muḥammad is his Messenger', the ṣalāt or liturgical prayer, zakāt or alms, fasting in the month of Ramadān or ṣaum, pilgrimage or ḥaǧǧ.[9] Holy war or ǧihād[10] is not among the personal duties of a Muslim. The foregoing are all that is specifically required of a righteous Muslim. Spiritual edification and a life of contemplative prayer are not included in these duties. There is of course a term, duᶜā, for petitionary prayer.[11] And there are petitions, made even to Muḥammad and pious forefathers. But they do not belong to official Islam. The printed prayers are counted rather as occasional literature.[12] The theologically-educated Muslim is more interested in how petitionary prayer relates to predestination or qaḍāʾand qadar.[13], to the predestined date of death or aǧal,[14] and to the alteration of God's will or badāʾ.[15] This may be very interesting theologically and a spur to subtle deductions, but contemplative piety is hardly possible in the process.

Al Ghazālī says of prayer in his Iḥyāʾ Ulūm ed-Dīn (2 : 298): 'If you say, what is the point of petitionary prayer, when there is no avoidance of predestination (qaḍāʾ), know this: the rejection of temptation belongs to predestination, for petition is a spur (sabab) to rejection of temptation and to the inculcation of mercifulness, just as a shield encourages the deflection of an arrow and water encourages the emergence of plants from the earth. Just as the shield deflects the arrow in their mutual encounter, so petitionary prayer and temptation affects one another, and it is not part of belief in Divine predestination to bear no weapons – as the Koran says (Sura 4 : 71–3): "Believers, be ever on your guard" – or to provide no water once the seed has been sown, because people think: if growth is predetermined the seed will grow, but not otherwise. Rather the encouragement is connected with that which is encouraged; that is the first determination, which is like a moment – or even shorter.

The disposition of whatever the varied pattern of one's impulsions decrees occurs in stages and follows one's estimates: qadar assesses the good (qaddar) in accordance with an impulse, and rejects the bad inasmuch as it rejects it in accordance with an impulse[16] ... Petitionary prayer promotes the presence of the heart with God, and that is the aim of worship. Therefore the Prophet says: 'Petition is the essence of worship. In most cases the hearts of creatures are turned towards thought of God only when overwhelmed by need and dire affliction. If evil afflicts man, then he makes many petitions. For need impels to prayer and petition impels the heart towards God in humility and obedience. It is thus that remembrance (ḏikr) comes about, and that is the highest form of worship. Hence the Prophet, then the Saints, then (the ordinary) people, in that order, are subjected to trial because the heart is brought by need and humility to God and prevented from forgetting Him"...' (cf. Mt. 6; 8 : 32).

Works too are largely relegated to outward observance. There is of course an instruction that they are to be performed with the right intention (nīya).[17] But that too is a prescription of the correct, concnentrated performance of specific formal observances. The calendar, for instance, says of niya: at 5.55 a.m. nīya; at 6.00 a.m., prayer; and so on.

That is inadequate in the long run, especially in times of private and public tribulation. Does jurisprudence, the interpreter of the revealed Law, offer anything better? The following is an example from a classical Ḥanafite legal work, SarMab 9 : 58,7: 'A man hires a woman in order to commit an unchaste act and commits it. According to Abū Hanīfa they are not both subject to ḥadd-punishment.[18] Abū Yūsuf, Šaibānī and Šāfigī say: both are subject to ḥadd-punishment because the act of unchastity was committed by both of them, for hire does not render the use of the sexual organs legal, and is therefore of no account, just as much as if he paid her to cook or to bake bread, and then committed unchastity with her. This is so because the object of hire is a benefit (manfaᶜa) which is legally classifiable as property. And that which is achieved or aimed at through sexual intercourse is classifiable as satisfaction (ᶜitq) (of a duty or an impulsion), and of its nature that is not a property; and a contract without an object (maḥall) is on principle to be accounted as invalid. If therefore no contract has been made, the contract and permission are one and the same; if he enjoyed her illegitimately on the basis of her permission, he would be subject to ḥadd-punishment. But Abū Ḥanīfa argues from two traditions which he takes from Omar (i.e., the second Caliph): 1. A woman asked a shepherd for a drink. He refused to give her anything to drink unless she let him have his will of her. Omar spared both of them from ḥadd-punishment. 2. A woman asked a man for some thing. He refused to give her whatever it was unless she allowed him to have his will of her. Omar declined to administer ḥadd-punishment, declaring: 'This is a marriage-price'. But one may not say that she was spared the ḥadd-punishment because she found herself in a forced situation in which she feared that she would suffer thirst, for this interpretation does not require that he should be spared ḥadd-punishment. For there is no case of necessity for him if she requested some thing of value, as is shown in the second tradition, because he gave the following as cause (ᶜilla): 'This is a marriage-price'; in other words, the marriage-price and price of hire approximated to one another, for the Koran (4 : 24–8; Paret) says: 'Give them their dowry for the enjoyment of them you had [in marital intercourse] as a duty!' God calls the mah (marriage-price) aǧr (the price of hire). And if he said: 'I shall give you such and such a dowry if you commit unchastity with me', then ḥadd-punishment would not apply. The same is true if he says: 'I take you into service'. The reason is as follows: this action is not unchastity. The philologists do not call intercourse which depends on a contract unchastity, and distinguish unchastity from anything else only on the basis of the contract. Similarly they do not make any distinction between isti ǧār (hire) and nikāh (marriage), because the difference between them is legal and the philologists do not acknowledge it. Therefore we know that this action is not to be equated literally with zinā' (unchastity). Therefore there is an unclear state of affairs (šubha) with regard to the nullity of the binding nature of ḥadd-punishment, in order to fulfil the Divine Law; similarly, ḥadd-punishment does not apply to a muhtalis (someone who pilfers) for his action is not literally sariqa (theft). The explanation is as follows: what is aimed at in sexual intercourse, if it is also categorized as ᶜitq (liberation), is really a benefit, and the contract of service (isti ǧār) is legally intended for the possession of the benefit, and in view of this fact the state of affairs is unclear (59) in contradistinction to the duty to cook and bake. Further, the contract in this instance does not refer to what is aimed at in sexual intercourse, nor to any impulsion thereto; and the contract which refers to an object (maḥall) produces an unclear state of affairs in regard to this object, not in regard to another object'. – Is this an appropriate answer for a sinner tormented in conscience, and intent on avoiding punishment in the next world?

Since the earliest days of Islam, therefore, some Muslims have stressed and put into practice the emotional and sympathetic side of their religion. Since there is no official pastoral practice to take care of this aspect, there is a danger of this kind of piety developing in the margins of legality. From time to time its relation to revelation may have to be reconsidered in order to ensure the exclusive authority of revelation. Since time immemorial this tendency has been known as asceticism and/or mysticism (taṣawwuf)[19], after the woollen garment, or ṣūf, which these people wear as a kind of uniform.

In any case there are official Islamic theologians (such as Al-Ġhazālī[20]) who represent a devotional Islam that extends beyond pure dogmatic theology and legality. It is attributed entirely to the mystics; sometimes that does seem to be the case, but it is not always so if we understand mysticism properly. Essentially it is the unio mystica (to be attained to by means of a minutely-established gradus), with theological and ethical consequences: for instance, an un-Islamic monism, whereas what was taught and practised by Al-Ġhazālī and his like was rather a kind of pietism which emphasized distance from God, creatureliness, conviction of sinfulness and conversion as essential for a pious death[21] – there is hardly any mention of a pious life. The main sources are Al-Ġhazālī's Ihyāᶜ Ulum ed–Din (The Revivification of the Sciences by Religion) (the fourth part, 'The Saving Qualities' [munǧiyāt] is relevant to the present topic) and works more or less dependent on him.[21a] The Ihya contains a detailed chapter on hope (raǧā) (VI; 123ff), which I shall refer to more closely. The arrangement of the book makes it seem as if this section belonged to a mystico-ascetical treatise. On closer examination, however, it is shown to have been originally a pietistic amplification of a dogmatically and legally impoverished Islam. As far as the composition of the work as a whole is concerned, it should be remembered that Al-Ġhazālī had a predecessor in this regard: Al-Makkī, 'Qūt al-qulūb', who was in fact a mystic.[21b]

Ġhazālī saw that correct tauḥīd (profession of unity) and a disciplined conduct of life did not in themselves conduce to fear of death, and thus did not promote a life lived in fear and trembling of the judicium speciale after death and the judicium generale after the resurrection. A psychologist of religion, such as William James, would say that it was a case of specially-disposed individuals, who are however not so infrequently met with and who require an emotional supplement to established religious practice, particularly in Islam which has no official pastoral care. There is no question here of an original mystical treatise, as is shown by the many anecdotes of the deaths of pious Muslims inserted into the relevant chapter. Meditation on hope is not the prerequisite here for further mystical stages or conditions, but a kind of consolation when dying for a sensitive, pious Muslim who risks falling into a conviction of loss of salvation. Only later were these meditations included in the mystical treatise – as a kind of elevation of the via negativa; retrospectively, they were attributed to mysticism in regard to the whole complex, even though in the strict sense it was only a kind of preparation.

Al-Ġhazālī first explains what hope really is:[22] 'Know: hope belongs among the "stations" of the "pilgrim" (sālikūn) and among the "states" of the "seeker" (ṭālibūn). The quality is only called a "station" if it is firm and solid. It is only called a state (ḥāl) if it is arbitrarily and quickly transient... Similarly with the distribution of the qualities of the heart... the unsettled is unknown as ḥāl (state)... Hope consists fully of state, knowledge and action. Knowledge is a spur which produces the state; the state requires action; and rǎḡa' is a name for the state of all three. The explanation is as follows: Everything which partakes of pleasant and unpleasant is divided into present, past and future. If something past occurs to you, that is called memory and remembrance (ḏikr, taḏakkur); if something present, it is known as wağd, ḏauq and idrāk (manifestation, taste, perception); wağd, because it is a state which you discover in your soul.[23] If something future occurs to you and overcomes your heart (124), that is known as intiẓār and tawaqquᶜ (expectation and prospect). If the expected is something unpleasant (makrūh) which produces anguish in the heart, then it is known as ḫauf and išfāq (fear and concern). But if it is something pleasant (maḥbūb), whose expectation... brings joy and pleasure to the heart, that joy is known as hope (rağā'). For hope means joy of the heart on account of the expectation of something which it finds pleasant. But this something pleasant which is expected must necessarily have an impulse. If its expectation comes about because of the occurrence of most of its impulses, then the term "hope" is appropriate to it. But if it is an expectation whose impulses are disturbed and upset, then the terms ġurūr and ḥumq (deception and foolishness) are more appropriate to it than hope. If it is not known precisely whether the impulses exist, then the term tamannī (wish) is more appropriate to expectation, for it is an expectation without cause.[24]

'In any case, the expression "hope and fear" is applied absolutely only to something with a certain variance (taraddud), but not to something that is definitely so. For no one says: "I hope for sunrise" when it is actually rising, and no one says: "I am afraid that it will go down" when it is actually going down, for that is definitely taking place. But one does say: "I hope that it will rain and I am afraid that it will stop".[25]

'The mystics or pietists (arbāb al-qulūb) know: that this world is the seedbed of the next world; that the heart corresponds to its ground, and faith to its seed therein; and the exercise of obedience to the irregularities and weeds in the ground, the digging of channels and the provision of water in them. The heart that carelessly depends on this world and is wholly taken up by it corresponds to the saliferous and unfruitful ground in which the seed will not grow. The day of the Last Judgment is the harvest day. There is harvest only when the seed has been sown. A crop grows only from the seed of faith, and seldom does a belief prove profitable along with an evil heart and the wickedness of its ways, just as no seed grows in a saliferous and unfruitful ground. Therefore one should measure human hope of forgiveness by (or treat it analogously with) the hope of the owner of the crop. For everyone who seeks good ground and sows good, unspoiled and faultless seed in it, nourishes it with what it needs; that is, provides water at the right time and weeds the ground; that is, removes thorns, useless vegetation and everything that prevents the seed from growing or spoils it; then sits and waits for bad weather and destructive catastrophes to be warded off by the graciousness of God, until the crop has fully ripened – everyone who does all that has an expectation which is called hope. But if anyone scatters the seed on hard ground permeated with saliferous water – ground situated high up so that no water can enter it –, does not care for the seed and then expects a harvest from it, he has an expectation which is called foolishness and deception. And if he scatters the seed on good land which however is devoid of water and then expects abundant rainwater where it hardly ever falls, and continues in this course (or: if the ground is not weeded), he has an expectation which is wishful thinking (tamannī), not hope (rağā'). For the term "hope" applies only to the expectation of something pleasant, for which all the impulses behind the human will are prepared and where only that is additional which does not come within the sway of one's will, in other words the bounty of God, in the shape of the deflection of alien catastrophes and damage; then the following happens to man: if he scatters the seed of faith, waters it with the water of obedient actions, clears the heart of the thorns of bad habits, expects of the bounty of God that He will strengthen him to the moment of his death, and shape his end well, which leads to forgiveness, then his expectation is real hope worthy of praise in its own right, which impels him wholly and constantly to do what is demanded by the impulsions of faith, in fulfilment of the movements of forgiveness, unto death. But if he ceases to nurture the seed of faith with the water of obedient actions or allows the heart to be burdened with bad habits, and wholly gives himself up to the pursuit of the pleasures of this life, then awaits forgiveness, his expectation is foolishness and deception (Koran 19 : 59–60; 7 : 169–168; 18 : 6, 33–4).

Accordingly, the man who strives in obedience and avoids sin is worthy to await the full grace of God's goodness, which consists in his being allowed entry to Paradise. If the sinner regrets and makes retribution for his previous failings, then he is worthy to hope to receive the gift of penitence. But in regard to the gift of penitence, if he condemns sin by blaming himself fundamentally and by most assiduously cultivating remorse, he is worthy to request from God assistance in becoming penitent; for his rejection of sin and his fierce desire for repentance correspond to the impulse that leads to repentence, and the assistance given consists only of the strengthening of that impulse' (Koran 2: 218–215).

125: Fear is not antithetical to hope, but associated with it.

'Koran 39 : 53–4: Do not despair of Allah's mercy! [God to Jacob]: "Do you know why I separated you and Joseph? Because you said: 'The wolf will eat him because You are not attentive'. Why did you fear the wolf and expect the neglect of his brothers, but not that I should look after him?" The Messenger of God: "No one may die without having a good opinion of God..."'

'The Messenger of God visited a dying man and said: "How are you?" He answered: "I find that I am afraid of my sins and hope in the mercifulness of my Lord". Then the Messenger of God said: "Both are not found together in a human heart in one place, without God giving him what he hopes for and preserving him from what he fears".'[26]

126 [Reproach of God's Messenger]: '"Why do you render man desperate?"

'After his death Yaḥyā b. Akṯam was seen in a dream.[27] Someone said to him: "What has God done with you?" He said: "God revealed Himself to me and said: 'You bad old man! You have done this and that!' Then I was filled with such terror as only God can tell. Then I said: 'O Lord! I have not related such a thing of You'. He: 'And what have you related of Me?' I: '... Gabriel: You have said: I am as my servant suspected I was. Therefore he may suspect what he will of Me! I have always suspected that You would not punish me'. Then God said: 'Gabriel told you the truth'."

126: 'An Israelite was wont to throw people into despair and to make it difficult for them. On the Day of Resurrection God will say to him: "Today I shall let you despair of My mercifulness, just as you allowed My servants to despair of it".'

127: 'Know: this one of two men is in need of this means of salvation [of hope]: either he who is overcome by despair and therefore neglects worship, or he who is overcome by fear and thereupon surrenders himself wholly to worship until he injures himself and his family. These two men both deviate from due proportion to the two extremes of inadequacy and excess. Hence they require a means of salvation that will restore them to due proportion. As for the sinner who deceives himself and fosters desires contrary to God, together with neglect of worship and abandonment to sin, on his account the saving means of hope change into deadly poisons... No, rather nothing but the saving means of fear should be applied to the deceived' [advice to popular preachers to follow this course.]

128: 'The Messenger of God said: My umma is a community which is shown mercy, which in the next world receives no punishment, to which in this world God accords its punishment in the form of earthquake and unrest. When the Day of Resurrection comes, a Jew of a Christian will be allotted to every man of my community and then it will be said: "This is your ransom from the fire".' (In Shi'ite works fanatical Sunnites are treated thus[28]).

129: 'If man commits a sin and asks God for forgiveness, God says to His angels: "Look at My servant who has committed a sin and knows that he has a Lord Who forgives sins and Who prosecutes on account of sin. I hereby call you to witness that I have forgiven him"... "If My servant were to sin until his sins reached to the clouds in the sky, I would forgive him as long as he asked Me for forgiveness and hoped in Me..." '[29]

130: 'Someone came to the Prophet saying: "Envoy of God! I fast only for the month of Ramaḍān, but no more. I pray only the Five Prayers, but no more. And I offer God no alms from my property and no pilgrimage and no additional work. Where shall I go when I die?" Then God's Envoy smiled and said: "Indeed, you will be with me if only you guard your heart from two things: from hatred (ġill) and envy (ḥasad), and your tongue from two things: from calumny and lies, and your eyes from two things: from looking at what God has forbidden, and from despizing a Muslim with both eyes: then you will enter Paradise with me by these two hands of mine".'

131: 'He whose last words are Lā ilāha illā' Llāh (There is no god apart from God) will not be touched by the fire, and he who meets God without having associated any thing with Him, will not be touched by the fire...

'A preacher should mix fear with hope. – God rejoices at being able to forgive.'

132: 'The Envoy of God: "His works will bring none of you into Paradise and save you from the fire". They said: "Not even you, Envoy of God?" He answered: "Not even me, unless God has covered me with His mercy..." '[30]

132 (middle): 'ᶜAli: "Whoever commits a sin and has it covered by God in this world, finds that God is too generous to reveal it in the next world. If someone commits a sin and is punished for it in this world, finds that God is too just to repeat His punishment for His servant in the next world". God permits no ᶜiṣma (sinlessness), because otherwise no forgiveness would be possible'.[31]

133: 'This shows that service of God in hope is better, for love is of greater weight for the one who hopes than for the one who is afraid. What a difference there is among kings between the one who serves him because he hopes for his goodness and his magnanimity!' – Fear is always coupled with hope,[32] sometimes even in the same chapter.[33] I cite an example from a modern Shi'ite work, Āmilī, 1f (cf. bibliography, n. 1):

'Fear of God (ittiqā') has four stages:

'1. ḫauf (fear). Allah's scourge by means of which he encourages those who flee His gate and brings them over the "bridge", until by that means the affairs of those are settled whose reason is conquered by the assuagement of suffering, averted by their action in practising circumspection. It is characterized by long lamentation and hopelessness.

'2. ḫašya (anguish). This is the illumination of the heart by which one sees what is good and evil within one; the bridle of knowledge which keeps the soul from injustice and sin. It is characterized by lasting self-observation in secret and in public. It occurs only after great patience and much knowledge (Koran 35 : 31–28).

3. 'haiba (respect). His prince is a king who dwells only in every repentant heart searching for forgiveness and only stays in the court of every penitent convert, so that it is said: whenever respect is separated from a heart, it perishes. It is characterized by migration to the gate of Divine mystery and long, thirsty sojourn under the cloud of goodness and the burning from the soul of the lodgings of the passions.

'4. rahba (awe). It signifies a definite inclination to flight. But the one who thus takes flight, always flees because he expects punishment on account of his shameful characteristics, and the following are among his traits and characteristics: frustration of the heart from within, his flight, his arousal from enlightenment until he attains almost to a state of inward awe with an afflicted and sombre exterior...'[34] According to ᵉAmili (8) there are also four modes of hope:

1. hope in the reception of good works;
2. hope in the reception of contrition at bad works;
3. hope in the future reception of grace, so that good and bad deeds are not balanced and mingled; perhaps God will forgive one's bad actions and not cancel one's good deeds; that is the hope of believers...
4. hope in permanent forgiveness despite one's inadequacies, which is a deceptive and deceitful form of hope. Whoever knows that his soul is bad must be anxious, downcast and fearful, but not hopeful...'

The jurists were also able to use this approach in order to interiorize jurisprudence to some extent. One example of this tendency is al-Fanārī, who died in 1431.[35]

With him I close this account of the pastoral treatment of fear and hope as preparation for a happy end. Al-Ghazālī said in principle all that was to be said on the subject, but he also made some remarks on fear and hope within the treatise on mysticism:

135a: 'Know: fear is an expression for the pain and burning of the heart from expectation of something unpleasant in the future. This was already made clear in the explanation of the reality of hope. Whoever is intimate with God and whose heart is possessed by God (al-ḥaqq), who becomes the son of his "times" [cf. Hartmann, pp. 81–3] and perceives forever the beauty of God (al-ḥaqq), is devoid of reference to the future. No fear and no hope remain, but his state is higher than fear and hope. Both are reins which prevent the sould from advancing to levity.' al-Wāsitī refers to this in these words: 'Fear is a curtain between God and man'.

He also says: 'If God (al-ḥaqq) appears to him above mysteries, then he does not retain the virtue of hope or the virtue of fear. By and large, if the lover busies his heart with the contemplation of the beloved, fearing separation, this is inadequate contemplation. The permanency of contemplation alone is the goal of the stations...'

The scales or treatises are not uniform. I cite one from a Shi'ite commentary on Al Ghazālī's Iḥyā ᶜUlūm ad-dīn by al-Kāšānī, VII, 286–7:

'The maqāmāt (stages or stations):

'al-yaqīn (certainty) is an expression for the strength of belief in God, the Last Day, Paradise, and the fire.

'This yaqīn awakens fear of the fire and hope in Paradise.

'Fear and hope empower one to the point of composure (ṣabr). ṣabr leads to mugāhada (inward struggle) (against impure desires), concentrated thought of God and lasting consideration of Him.

'Lasting contemplation leads to full knowledge (gnosis). Gnosis and intimacy lead to love.'

'Then follow the stages of contentment (riḍā'), confidence in God (tawakkul), and the other maqāmāt.[36]

Fear and hope are to be prescribed only in the proportions Al-Ghazālī recommends, for otherwise they render one incapable of living, and that certainly does not accord with true Islam, which always teaches one to observe due proportion. But both terms are essential because they remind the Muslim: tua res agitur! In addition they tell him that the creature (the ᶜabd) has no legal claim upon his Creator (cf. Lk. 17 : 10). Absolute certainty of salvation and damnation[37] does not fit the created status of human existence as understood in Islamic anthropology.

## Notes

1 On hope in Christianity, see Feiner & Vischer (Eds), The Common Catechism (London, 1975) and A New Catechism (London, 1969), references in indexes. The term is used more often and more intensively by Christians. The probable reasons are: the doctrine of original sin (a greater degree of lostness which requires greater assistance); the death and resurrection of Jesus Christ; the sacraments. Stieglecker, pp. 569ff; the term is not in the index. Cf. also André-Jean Festugière, OP, Ursprünge christlicher Frömmigkeit (Freiburg im Breisgau, 1963), esp. pp. 91ff: 'Der Mönch und das Fasten' (the monk and fasting).

2 See under īmān.

3 This occurs under other headwords in eschatology: the sign of the hour/ašrāt al-sāᶜa; the return of Jesus/ᶜĪsā; Daǧǧal (HWI: Dadjdjāl); Mahdī.

4 The explanations of all Suras derive from Baiḍāwi.

5 Later in Islamic history there are approaches to ecclesiasticization, see Gibb/Bowen I/2, p. 72 ('universal Church') in section pp. 70ff: 'The religious institutions'. But see Ernst S. Hirsch, 'Laizismus (Layiklik) als verfassungsrechtlicher Begriff in der Türkischen Republik', in: Orient 15 (1074), pp. 106–12 and 173; II, end: 'Moreover the appellant (a political party) referred to the fact that in Islam there is no priestly caste ('ruhbanlik'); if an appropriate group of officials were formed, one would create a priestly caste ('ruhban sinifl'), which would be to strike a blow against the principles of Islam'. The following section III (basis of the judgment) shows clearly that according to Turkish constituional law Islam has not developed a Church.

6 See Gottschalk, p. 27; Muzaffar: only one chapter on piety and prayer/duᶜā'; see EI[2], under ᶜaḳīda.

7 See HWI, under Djahm b. Ṣafwan.

8 See Naraqi, 214 : 3.

9 See HWI, under Ḥadjdi.

10 See HWI, under Djihād.

11 See EI[2].

12 Padwick, IXff, pp. 178–9; 201ff.

13 See HWI, under Ḳaḍā'and Ḳadar.

14 See EI[2] under Adjal.

15 See EI[2].

16 Cf. Kulaini, pp. 466, 469–70: bāb al-duᶜā'yarudd al-balā'wal-qaḍā'.

17 See HWI.

18 See LIW, under criminal law.

19 See HWI under Tarīḳa.

20 See EI[2] under Al-Ghazālī.

21 As an example of mystical thought, cf. Sarrag, p. 92: (He who hopes appropriately) hopes for nothing from God apart from God.

21a There is therefore a specific ethics, partly nourished from non–Islamic sources.

21b There is also a kind of gradus or 'ladder of perfection' in Nonconformist devotion; see, e.g., John Bunyan's The Pilgrim's Progress.

22 On the terms fear and hope, see Naraqi, pp. 195ff (ḫauf), 213ff (rağā'); Dailami, pp. 139ff (bāb 28), 143ff (bāb 29: Rağā'); Muhasibi, pp. 120ff 23; Kulaini, pp. 68ff; Makki, pp. 443 bewlos, 444, 446, 450, 454, 456, 458; Qummi, p. 83; Amili, p. 9.

23 Therefore not ecstasy here.

24 For the dinstiction between rağā' and tamannī, see Gauziya, pp. 298–301.

25 Cf. Narqi, p. 210.

26 Cf. Naraqi, p. 443.

27 In the last book of Iḥyā ᶜUlūm ed-dīn: ḏikr al-maut/meditatio mortis wa-mā baᶜdahū, there are three sections on dreaming of the dead, ch. 8.9. 10 (VI, pp.430–6).

28 See Maraqi, p. 229.

29 Cf. Makki, p. 435 above.

30 Cf. Maglisi 385–45 = 389 : 54 middle; Makki, 448 below; Saffarini, p. 281 (taufīq, ḫiḏlān); Asqalani, pp. 50, 51; Kulaini, pp. 71/2 : 1.

31 See Makki, p. 434 : 12.

32 See the image of the two wings of the bird; he can only fly with both wings. Dailami, p. 45 below; Misbah, bāb, p. 88.

33 See Naraqi, p. 223; Maglisi, pp. 323–401; 352 : 1; 323–52; the relevant Suras; 352–401: the relevant ḥadīṯh; Makki, pp. 438, 443–4.

34 Cf. Maglisi, p. 360 above, 372 : 22; 380 : 30; 382 : 34.

35 See E. Gräf, 'Vom Geiste islamischen Rechts', in: Festschrift für Ernst Klingmüller (Karlsruhe, 1974), pp. 126ff.

36 See also Narqi, p. 214; Qusairi, pp. 31/2, 45ff, 59ff (ḫauf), 62ff (rağā'), 69ff (ḥuzn); Hartmann, pp.24–5; Maglisi 372–3, 374 : 19; Makki, pp. 364, 443–4; Sarrag, pp. 65ff.

37 Maglisi, p. 377 : 22: from fear of the last judgment, someone caused himself to be burned after death, and one half of the ashes to be scattered at sea and the other half on dry land. God collected them all together and forgave him.

# Bibliographical abbreviations


| | |
|---|---|
| Amili | Muḥammad al-ᶜAinātī al-ᶜĀmili, Ādāb al-nafs, part 2 (Teheran, 1380). |
| Asqalani | Ibn Ḥaǧar al-ᶜAsqalānī, al-Istiᶜdād li-yaum al-maᶜād (Beirut, 1972). |
| Baidawi | Baidāwi, Anwār al-tanzīl wa-asrār al-ta'wīl (Cairo, 1330). |
| Dailami | al-Dailami, Irv-sād al qulūb (n.p., 1375?). |
| EI² | Encyclopaedia of Islam, new edition (Leiden & London, 1960ff). |
| Feiner-Vischer | Johannes Feiner & Lukas Vischer (Eds), The Common Catechism (London, 1975). |
| Gauziya | Ibn Qaiyim al-Ǧauzīya, Kitāb al-rūḥ (Hyderabad. ³1357). |
| Ghazali | Abū Ḥāmid...al-Ġhazālī, Iḥyāʾ ᶜUlūm ed-dīn, 4 vols (Cairo, 1334); McKane, Al-Ghazali's Book of Fear and Hope, ET with intro. and indices (London, 1962); G.-H. Bousquet, Ihya ᶜouloum ad-din, ou vivification des sciences de la foi (Paris, 1955) (analytical index). |
| Gibb/Bowen | H.A.R. Gibb & Harold Bowen, Islamic Society and the West: A Study of the impact of western civilization on Moslem culture in the Near East, vol. I/2 (London, 1957). |
| Gottschalk | H.-L. Gottschalk, 'Der Islam. Seine Entstehung, Entwicklung und Lehre', in: Franz König, Christus und die Religionen (Vienna & Freiburg, ²1961), pp. 3–72. |
| Hartmann | Richard Hartmann, Al-Ḳuschairī's Darstellung des Sufitums (Berlin, 1914). Cf. Qusairi. |
| NC | A New Catechism (London, 1969) (the 'Dutch Catechism). |
| HWI | Handwörterbuch des Islam, eds. A.J. Wensinck & J.H. Kramers (Leiden, 1941). |
| James | William James, The Varieties of Religious Experience (New York & London, 1902). |
| Kasani | Maulā Muḥsin al-Kāšāni, al-Maḥaǧǧa al-baiḍā' fi tahḏīb al-iḥyā', part 7 (Teheran, 1342 s). |
| Koran | The Koran, trans. N.J. Dawood, fourth revised edition (Harmondsworth, 1974). Suras numbered in accordance with the official Egyptian edition. |
| Kulaini | al-Kulainī, al-Uṣūl min al-Kāfī, part 2 (Teheran, 1375/1335). |
| LIW | Lexikon der islamischen Welt, 3 vols. (Stuttgart, 1974). |
| Maglisi | Muḥammad Bāqir al-Maǧlisī, Biḥār al-anwār, 70th part (Teheran, 1386 q). |
| Makki | Abū Tālib Muḥammad b. ᶜAli b. ᶜAṭīyā al-Ḥāriṯi al-Makki (d. 386); Qūt al-qulūb fī muᶜāmalāt al-maḥbūb wa-waṣf ṭarīq al-murīd ilā maqām al-mufīd, part I (Cairo, 1381/1961). |
| Misbah | Gaᶜfar b. Muḥammad al-Ṣādiq, Miṣbāḥ al-šarīᶜa (n.p., n.d.). |
| Mhasibi | Josef van Ess, Die Gedankenwelt des Ḥāriṯ al-Muḥāsibī (Bonn, 1961). |
| Muhammad | b. Muḥammad al-Ḥusaini al-Zabīdī al-Murtaḍā, Itḥāf al-sāda al-muttaqin bi-šarḥ asrār iḥyā ᶜulūm al-dīn, part 9 (Beirut, 1301). |
| Muzaffar | Muḥammad Riḍā al-Muẓaffar, ᶜAqā'id al-imāmīya (Naǧaf, n.d.). |
| Naraqi | Muhammad Mahdi al-Naraqi (d. 1209), Gami al-sa adat, I (Nagaf, n.d.). |
| Padwick | Constance E. Padwick, Muslim Devotion. A study of prayer manuals in common use (London, 1961). |
| Qummi | Ibn Bābūya al-Qummī, Muḥammad b. ᶜAli, Ǧāmi ᶜal-aḫbār kāšif al-asfār (Mašhad, n.d.). |
| Qusairi | al-Qušairi, al-Risāla al-qušairīya fīᶜilm al-taṣawwuf (Cairo, 1957/1367). |
| RGG | Die Religion in Geschichte und Gegenwart (Tübingen, ³1956). |
| Saffarini | al-Saffārīnī, Lawāʾiḥ al-anwār al-bahīya wa-sawāṭi ᶜal-asrār al-aṯariya, part 1 (Cairo, 1323. Commentary on his work: al-Durra al-muḍīʾa fi |

| | |
|---|---|
| | ‘aqd al-firqa al-mardiya (GAL SII, 449 : 8 : Mas‘ud b. ‘A. Rida is not the commentator). |
| SarMab | al-Saraḫsī, K. al-Mabsūṭ, 30 parts (Cairo, 1324–31). |
| Stieglecker | Hermann Stieglecker, Die Glaubenslehren des Islam (Paderborn, 1962). |
| Sarrag | al-Sarrāǧ (d. 378), Kitab al-lumaʿ fi l-taṣawwuf (Cairo, 1380/1960). |

# Principles of Religious Education in Present-Day Islam

*Michael Winter*

I realize that to some extent my topic lies outside the main lines of this colloquium. The other contributions have to do with the substance of the monotheistic religions; they are concerned with theological, cultural and philosophical questions and contribute to a better understanding of these religions. I, on the other hand, examine not the question of what modern Islam signifies, but only how Islam is taught today in the schools of some Arabic countries and in Turkey. My findings are based on the textbooks and curricula of Egypt, Jordan, Syria and Turkey, and on personal experiences and observations in Arab society and in Arab education in Israel and on the West Bank.

I should like to stress that the main theme of my investigation (textbooks) has significant advantages, but also limitations. An examination of religious textbooks provides us with no clear and authoritative picture of modern Islam. It does not even allow us a definitive understanding of the ultimate product of the schools: the spiritual and religious world of the pupil. Every educator is well aware that textbooks do not always offer an exact image of what is taught in the classroom. Finally, the school is not the only and perhaps not the main factor which decides the child's understanding of the world.

On the other hand the official educational policy is most clearly reflected in textbooks and curricula.

Authorities are in a position to evade controverted issues by means of ambiguous explanations. But in the textbook which the pupil receives everything must be stated clearly and unequivocally. Therefore textbooks are the best indication of the kind of Islam the authorities are concerned to propagate. This applies to all countries, but especially to totalitarian régimes where the educational authorities not only approve but indeed prepare and issue the books.

The authors of textbooks are almost exclusively inspectors and teachers and many of these books are written by committees appointed by ministries of education.

It must be stressed that instruction in the Islamic faith in its present-day form, as a subject in its own right, is something new, and only began in the period of modernization, that is, about a hundred years ago. Not so long ago the only educational institution for children in the Muslim world of the Near East was the kuttāb, that is, the Koranic school which, incidentally, corresponds to the Jewish heder or cheder. Schooling as a whole consisted only of subjects of a religious nature, such as the Koran, the history of the Prophet, dogma and cultic instruction, both in the kuttāb and at the higher levels. In the kuttāb the main emphasis was on learning the Koran by heart. Most important of all was word-by-word repetition and not independent thought and the ability to express oneself.[1]

The autobiography of the great Egyptian writer and thinker, Ṭāhā Ḥussein, contains the classic description of the system. As a pupil Hussein experienced all the inadequacies of this system, and as minister of education tried to change and to improve it.[2]

As a result of the modernization of society and of the near-eastern states, the representatives of religion lost their monopoly over education, and today the dominant form of education in these countries is the modern state school with its secular orientation. Children in private schools are also taught in accordance with the general principles. The curriculum of these official schools allows for about three hours of religious instruction every week. Religious education is universally compulsory (although the number of hours given to it is not the same in all countries).

Turkey, as is well-known, is the only state in the Near East in which the state and religion are constitutionally separate. Secularism is no longer so strictly observed as in Atatürk's time. In the first years of the Republic religion was not taught at all in the schools. In the 1940s children received religious instruction only at their parents' request. When the Democratic Party took over the government in 1950 the relation to religion, including religious education, changed. Since then all children receive it, with the exception of those whose parents request their exemption.[3]

For comparison's sake, I should add that in Israel, where I come from, in contradistinction to the Islamic countries, there is no subject known as religious education or instruction. We have religious and non-religious schools. In both types subjects are taught which are elements of the Jewish religion, such as the

Bible and the Talmud. The difference consists in the nature of the instruction and in the atmosphere of the school. In the non-religious schools the Bible is taught from a literary-historical standpoint. In the religious schools it is taught along traditional religious lines. The parents choose the type of school for their children.

In Islam as in Judaism the main stress is on the fulfilment of religious duties. Dogmas are of course important too, but merely in second place. Traditionally, Judaism recognizes 613 religious commandments, many more than Islam which in the Koran already stresses that it does not wish to overburden its faithful.[4]

This categorial difference is very important for our present deliberations. Jewish religious instruction educates in faith and also in an all-inclusive form of life. Present-day Islamic education places more emphasis on the experience of belonging to the community than on the form taken by everyday religious, individual feeling and life.

In the territories I discuss Islam is dependent on the state. The religious leaders and institutions, even those which like the Azhar University in Cairo, enjoy particular prestige, are controlled by the state authorities, so that, even if they wished to do so, they are not in a position decisively to influence the nature of religious education.[5]

Islam as taught nowadays in the countries I mentioned above, is 'modern Islam' in contradistinction to the understanding of 'fundamentalist conservative Islam'. There are indeed adherents of the latter viewpoint, but here it is a question of subterranean movements, such as the 'Muslim Brotherhood' in Egypt, or they can raise their voices only outside the borders of the countries mentioned – as is the case with Muᶜammar Qadhāfi, the President of Libya. Egypt, and to a lesser extent the other states, adopted Reform-Islam as their official ideology.

This rationalistic tendency gave rise at the end of the last, and at the beginning of the present, century to a movement under the leadership of Ǧamāl al-Dīn al-Afghāni and his successor Muḥammad Abdoh (1849-1905). The textbooks are especially fulsome in their praise of the personality and views of ᶜAbdoh, who became the Mufti for Egypt and introduced reforms into the al-Azhar University.[6]

The main problem which ᶜAbdoh and other modernists encountered was that of the antithesis between Islam and 'reason and science'. ʿAbdoh asserted that there was in fact no such opposition.

The modernists taught that everything in Islam which gave the impression of backwardness was only a later decadent addition. Examination of original Islam showed that it was activist and rationalist in nature.[7]

There is no doubt that ʿAbdoh was loyal to Islam as well as to 'progress'. This attitude required an unhistorical interpretation of the original texts which however weakened their absolute, compulsive force. The result of the attitude I have described was a compromise between the demands of Islam and the twentieth century. This compromise is certainly marked by good will but is apologetically orientated at the same time.

The Islamic curricula contain four themes: 1. principles of belief; 2. cultic requirements; 3. the rules governing economic relations; 4. general moral education.

As far as the texts are concerned, the books contain sentences and chapters from the Koran and their explanation, and in addition Hadith, the prophetic tradition, or sayings concerning the behaviour of Muḥammad, historical texts which refer to his life history and the original development of Islam.

In general, we may say that in the first classes of the elementary schools there is an emphasis on belief in God, whereas the higher classes stress cultic requirements, and the highest classes questions of economic relations and of personal status (mainly marriage and divorce).[8] In these top classes much time is also devoted to discussions of general questions such as the solidarity of the Islamic nations, freedom in Islam, and the relation between religion and nationalism.[9] The Islam which the pupils learn is humanistic. All humanistic principles already existed in the classical period of Islam, but the subjection of man to God was valued more highly. In the past man's duties were placed before his rights. Earlier on cultic duties were stressed, but now the emphasis is on how easily they can be fulfilled.[10] All books stress the fact that Islam corresponds to human nature. Man is originally monotheistic, as is Islam. It acknowledges the sexual impulse and striving for possessions, satisfaction, freedom, knowledge and equality and takes into account excessive hardship. The author of the textbook for the first class of the Jordanian schools closes his exposition thus in order to show that Islam is universal and fits all times and all places.[11]

In his interesting study, Olivier Carré looks at the social, economic and political content of the Egyptian textbooks. He distinguishes the 'Islamic pole' from the 'social pole'. He tested the quantitative relation between the material dealing with society and the total content of the books, and found that this material was the greater part and continually increased in extent from the lower to the upper classes. In the third class, in which religious education begins, these topics account for 40% and in the highest class of the middle school 94%.[12]

The pupil receives general, not very detailed explanations of cultic requirements. He receives, sometimes with accompanying pictures, explanations of the way to pray, Ramadan usage, and pilgrimage to Mečca. He is told how he has to pray in Ǧihād (the holy war). In Jordan special weight is put on the correct liturgical recitation of the Koran.[13]

In the first years after the foundation of the Turkish Republic the textbooks contained nothing about worship. Nowadays pupils in Turkey too are given instruction on the cult and its ethical and symbolic value.[14]

In regard to economic relations, the books mention the fact that the Koran forbids the charging of interest.[15] There is no explanation of how a modern economy can be conducted without charging interest.

I shall now discuss the textbooks' treatment of specific religious questions.

Many books are inimical to Sufism, that is, Islamic mysticism.[16] They see it as one of the reasons for degeneration, contributing to passivity. The Sufis are said to have misunderstood the Islamic notions of asceticism and trust in God. Modern Islam would stress the fact that these concepts do not mean laziness and fatalism, as the Sufis interpreted them in practice. Nevertheless Sufism is not illegal in the Arab countries and some observers, such as Professor Morroe Berger, predict its renaissance.[17] In Turkey, on the other hand, the Sufist orders have been illegal since their rising in the Republic in 1925, and hence the textbooks there are much more inimical to the Sufis than in the Arab countries.

The question of sects within Islam is hardly mentioned in the textbooks. Shiᶜism is only curtly mentioned in Turkish schools as a danger for Islam in the context of the wars of the Ottoman Empire against the Shiᶜite Persians.[18] In Syria the textbooks are written with a Sunni emphasis and ignore the sects, even though the population there contains Shiᶜite sects. Even President Assad of Syria belongs to one of them. Jordan and Egypt do not have these problems to contend with.

In Egypt the relation of the state to Shariᶜa, the Islamic law, is quite modern in tendency. The religious courts were of course abolished. Religious law certainly still applies in matters of personal status, but operates only within the state legal framework. The government tries to unite all four schools of law. The pupil receives a detailed and careful explanation of the historical development of Islamic law and of the four schools and their characteristics. The textbook for the second middle-school class in Egypt says that the law of Islam is living and continues to develop, and yet the report stops at the year 1936 without giving the pupil any details of the important developments that have taken place since the Revolution.[19]

The distinctions between the four Islamic schools of law have lost their importance in the modern world, and the textbooks, even in the upper stages of educational institutions, do not elaborate on them.

The Jordanian curriculum advises the pupil not to go into these questions.[20] This is in the line of the modernists, as for example ᶜAbdoh, who wanted to unite the schools of law.

In regard to the differences between the four orthodox Islamic schools of law, it is interesting to discover that precisely in Turkey – where the whole question is theroretical (because Islamic law does not apply there) –, the theme is discussed in the textbook for seminaries. It mentions that the Hanafite school of law, which was the official Ottoman school of law, was rationalistic at a time when the other schools of law, especially the Malikite and Hanbalite, followed tradition and not reason.[21]

In all these countries the status of woman and family receives special attention. All books emphasize that Islam improved the state of woman in contradistinction to the pre-Islamic period. It educates one to respect for women and treats the family as the most important cell of a healthy society.

It is thought to be important that girls too should be educated. All the books mention the modesty and morality of women. Women are entitled to work outside the home, yet housekeeping and looking after children are their most important rôles.[22] A Syrian textbook opines that work outside the home does not contradict the natural constitution of women, apart from such occupations as politics and the law.[23]

The textbooks are not agreed on the question of polygamy. Egypt and Syria leave this problem out altogehter. Perhaps that is explicable by the general disappearance of polygamy in those countries. In Egypt polygamy is not absolutely forbidden, but the authorities condemn it so much that it is in fact almost out of the question.

It is interesting that the Jordanian textbook for the top class of secondary schools of all kinds unequivocally *supports* polygamy. The authors say that both Judaism and Christianity allowed it. The representatives of the Christian Church are said to have forbidden polygamy only in recent generations and to have permitted it in Africa up to today. The most important thing is that the Koran allows polygamy and that the Prophet had several wives. As is well-known, the Koran allows a man to marry four women, on the condition that he can treat all four of them with equal justice. The authors reject the modernists' objection that human nature excludes the possibility of behaving with equal justice to four wives. They justify polygamy for social, demographic and psychological reasons, and maintain that polygamy reduces the suffering of sick and barren women as well as prostitution. This viewpoint is to be explained not only by the fact that Jordan is more conservative than Egypt and Syria, but in that it is a country from which a large number of men emigrate, leaving an excess of women behind.[24]

Turkey, which adopted the Swiss Code civil in 1928, forbids polygamy. The fact that the Prophet had several wives makes it difficult for the authors of the present-day textbooks to justify monogamy. Somewhat apologetically, they explain that in the lifetime of his first wife Khadīǧa, the Prophet took no other wife. Only after her death did he take several wives, for political reasons and in order to give protection to war widows. The authors maintain that the Turkish monogamy law corresponds to Islam.[25]

The Egyptian textbooks take a positive standpoint as regards birth control. It is well-known that the population explosion is one of the most difficult problems facing Egypt. The authors quote President Nasser, who said that the high natural increase in population was holding progress back. He criticized the opinion, especially widespread in the country areas, that family planning is contrary to Islam. The textbook for the second class of the middle school quotes the Koran and Hadith in order to show that that is not the case.

In a sentence of the Koran (2 : 233) which says that mothers shall give suck to their children for two whole years if the father wishes, the authors find support for birth control. Moreover they cite the Prophet's sayings to show that the prevention of injury is more important than any advantage, and furthermore that necessity turns forbidden into permitted actions.[26] In this regard I should like to remark that the standpoint of Islam on this issue is not unequivocal.[26a] Theologians such as Al-Ghazālī, who died at the beginning of the twelfth century, and was perhaps the greatest thinker of Islam of all times, and Sheikh Maḥmūd Shaltūt, who was Mufti of Egypt under Nasser, permitted birth control under certain conditions.[27]

It is known that the Egyptian government, which has charge of the institutions of Islam, had no difficulty in obtaining from religious experts a ruling according to religious law in favour of birth control. It is obvious therefore that the textbooks offer no contradictory opinion. It is also known that the preachers of lower rank, who are conservative, sabotage this demographic policy in their Friday sermons.[28]

Much space is devoted to the question of the state and government within the framework of discussions on topics of a social and general nature. The theoreticians of government in Islam have always found it difficult to explain the contradiction between the ideals of Islam and political reality.[29] Islam, in contradistinction to Christianity, is a socio-political religion and therefore found this contradiction exceedingly problematic. As we can see from contemporary Islamic religious curricula and textbooks, this state of affairs has remained essentially the same.

As in earlier time, Islam desires the religious textbooks to cover a complete socio-political system as well as act as guides to faith and worship. The books often contain chapters with titles such as 'Government in Islam' or 'An Islamic form of government', and so on. Some of the ideals treated in such chapters are expressed in an extremely vague and general way. They maintain, for instance, that the state is necessary, that government must be righteous, that man must be free, without the freedom of the individual restricting the freedom of others.[30] These are principles which hardly anyone would object to, but it is not possible to escape the impression that the authors' political conceptions are still rooted in mediaeval Islam. Their world knows only rulers and ruled (ḥakīm versus maḥkūm), not citizens. Each of these groups, among which there should be solidarity, has its duties. The ruler has the duty of ensuring the well-being of the ruled, and they must obey the ruler. He has to be advised and be led by the principles of religion. Like all modernists since the last century the authors are keen on the early Islamic principle of consultation, shūra. But, consultation, however praiseworthy it may be, is no guarantee of a democratic decision, such as the modernists would wish. According to an Egyptian textbook, it is one of the rights of subjects to criticize the government by means of contributions to the press or proposals in the popular assembly, and so on.[31] There is no mention of how the ruler attains to his position, and how he is removed. It appears that the legitimacy of the government does not reside in the mode by which power is obtained but in the way in which the ruler operates thereafter, or above all in *that* he operates! With regard to the Islamic mode of government, these books offer the traditional distinction between laws given by God and those made by man. The Egyptian textbooks maintain that the former are better than the latter, which are obeyed only under compulsion.[32] Here it is clear that the Egyptian pupil, who lives in a country in which most laws derive from the government and not from the Shariᶜa, or holy Law, is subject to doubt. We find the same antithesis of Shariᶜa and human law in the Syrian textbooks, though in a significantly more emphatic form. The textbook for the upper class of secondary schools states that every government which is not based on the principles of the Koran should be rejected. The authors harshly criticize materialists and hypocrites who only appear to be faithful Muslims.[33] The polemical tone is inseparable from the fierce contention between the orthodox and the radicals about the position of Islam in Syria.

As is known, in the Syria of the 1960s a dispute broke out concerning the constitutional position of Islam in the state. The orthodox party did not succeed in achieving the recognition of Islam as the state religion of Syria, as is the case in some Muslim states. They obtained only an express ruling in the constitution that the head of state must profess the Islamic faith. Every attempt of the radicals to remove this ruling caused unrest.

In Turkey, where the Shariᶜa is no longer state law, the topic is not mentioned in the textbooks.

The Egyptian textbooks represent the official ideology of the government, 'Arab socialism', in an Islamic wrapping.[34] Much already has been written about Arab socialism and the textbooks offer no new interpretation. In Egypt there is indeed a political left wing, which would view the official ideology as true socialism, but the religious educators contradict this view. Ishtirākiyya ᶜArabiyya, Arabic socialism, is not Marxism. It does not recognize class warfare and requires the solidarity of social classes; it presumes that there will always be rich and poor and stresses the right to private property.[35] The books also criticize monopolism and easy acquisition of riches. They stress the social values contained in some religious conventions, for instance almsgiving, which is one of the five 'pillars of Islam'. The fast of Ramadan is intended to remind the rich that the poor often suffer from hunger. Pilgrimage to Mecca enjoins the same clothing and the same cultic observance on all.[36]

Both the Arab and the Turkish textbooks see it as their duty to be concerned with the most important ideology of the present Near East, nationalism. They maintain that there is no contradiction between nationalism and Islam, but that they complement one another.[37]

The rôle of the Turkish educators is more difficult than that of the Arabs. The Arab world and ethos and Islam are hardly distinguishable. The origin of Arab and Islamic history is almost one and the same. For the Arabs the religious language is the same as the national language; that is not the case for the Turks.

The authors of the Arab textbooks are well aware that many of those who shaped Islamic history and civilization were not Arab in origin. But they see them nevertheless as bearers of a common Arab-Islamic heritage. Personalities of the classical age, such as the Persian al-Ghāzalī, the Turk Fārābī and the Kurd Saladin, are treated as belonging to the Arab world by reason of culture and language.[39] The Arab textbooks manage this by speaking consistently of 'Arabs and Muslims'. The Arab religious textbooks rarely mention 'patriotism', vataniyya, but emphasize the national commitment of qavmiyya, which plays a central part especially in the Palestine question.[40]

It is extraordinary that Egyptian identity is hardly mentioned in these books. I should like to stress the fact yet again that I am discussing textbooks about religion, and not other books in which 'patriotism' is mentioned frequently.

The position of the Turks in regard to their place in Islam is more problematical. They explain that, in contradistinction to the Arabs, they had an important civilization before they adopted Islam. They are proud of the status they achieved in Islam. Here I should like to observe that the Arabs value highly what Islam has done for them, whereas the Turks stress *their* contribution to Islam.

All religious textbooks preach religious tolerance. They maintain that Ǧihād, holy war, was never offensive, and was used only in defence of religion. Islam is not to be propagated with force. The textbooks forbid the persecution of religious minorities.[41]

The books show a marked tendency to restrict polemics between Islam and Christianity. Considerable space is given in the books to the personality of Jesus, though of course in agreement with the Islamic notion that he was not the son of God but a prophet.[42] The pupil is told that the Christian religion is closest to Islam. The textbooks represent the famous Koranic verse on the praise of monks as praise of all Christians.[43]

Now I have to touch upon a painful topic: the way in which the Arab textbooks of religion teach hatred of the Jews. Muḥammad's conflict with the Arab Jews in seventh-century Arabia is a historical fact. It is true to say that all religions feature expressions of enmity against other religions, and Judaism certainly does so. We must ask however whether such material should appear in religious textbooks. The Arab-Israeli conflict is complicated enough politically; it does not need the addition of a religious dimension.

The most extreme anti-Jewish attitude is to be found in the Jordanian religious textbooks. The teacher's introduction at the end of the textbook for the eighth class says: 'The teacher has to connect the Prophet's life with the present day, especially in regard to sections about the duty of holy war and struggle against the Jews. In this way he will give the pupils a profound understanding of the danger to Islam and Muslims represented by the Jews, and that the only deliverance from their wickedness is to be found in their expulsion or destruction'.[44]

A Syrian religious textbook for the third class of the secondary school which appeared in 1972 says: 'Even if some Jews believed in Islam and were converted to it, that does not contradict the circumstance that the Jews are the most malicious enemies of the

Muslims because they believed that they alone were entitled to the Prophet'.[45]

Most attacks on the Jews and Israel appear in the Arab textbooks on history and civics.[46] Although I have not referred to these subjects in my contribution, it is obvious that they affect young people's attitude to Judaism by introducing religious antagonism into the political conflict – where it does not belong.

The authors of the textbooks could draw on the history of Islam for many examples of tolerance towards Jewish and Christian religious communities and individuals. In classical, that is, mediaeval Islam, there was nothing that might be called hatred of the Jews, although the status of Jews and Christians in the Islamic states was lower than that of Muslims.

Finally, I accept Carré's conclusion, that the religious textbooks have not succeeded in offering a synthesis of Islam and the modern world.[47] Nevertheless, I believe that the textbooks are successful in teaching the Islamic religion as such. If we consider the books themselves – apart from other influences – as a criterion, it is clear that the Islamic faith is handed on to the pupils in a living, modern and non-dogmatic form. The religious texts of the Koran and Hadith are introduced to the pupil in an attractive way. The historical material which is so important in Islamic education makes instruction a vivid experience. The lack to which Carré draws attention is not an inadequacy of Islam, but the lack of success of the modernist attempt to adapt Islam to continually changing circumstances.

The principles of Islam as represented in the textbooks under discussion cannot be made fully to accord with present-day social and political conditions. At the same time we have to remember that even in the Middle Ages Muslim thinkers were trying without success to defend the fiction that the contemporary political state of affairs exactly corresponded to religious requirements.

Educators have achieved the best results in areas where they do not feel bound to adapt Islamic principles to the changing requirements of the authorities. Islam as a world-view and as educational material is taught most naturally and effectively when it summons men to believe in God and his messengers, identity with Islamic history, and solidarity with the community.

# Notes

1 See I. Goldziker, 'Education (Muslim)', in: Encyclopaedia of Religion and Ethics, V (1912), pp. 158-207.

2 Tāhā Ḥussein, al-Ayyām (Cairo, 1964), I, pp. 28-78.

3 See my article: M. Winter, 'Instruction in the Islamic Religion in the Republic of Turkey', in: Ha-Mizraḥ He-Ḥadash, XVIII, 3-4 (1968), pp. 223-45 (Hebrew).

4 Koran, 22 : 78.

5 See, e.g., D. Crecelius, 'al-Azhar in the Revolution', in: Middle East Journal XX (1966), pp. 31-49.

6 Y. al-Ḥamādī & M. ʿAṭā, al-Tarbiya al-Dīniyya (religious education for the third class of the secondary school) (Cairo, 1971), pp. 162-81; A.ᶜal-Sā'ih (et al.), Nahǧ al-Islām (Religious education for the second class of the secondary school) (Amman, 1968), pp. 254-63.

7 Cfl. Albert Hourani, Arabic Thought in the Liberal Age, 1768-1939 (London, 1962), pp. 103–60.

8 See, e.g., M. Barāniq (et al.), al-Tarbiya al-Dīniyya (Religious education for the second class of the secondary school) (Cairo, 1967), II, pp. 135–69.

9 Ibid., pp. 64–77; Religious education for the second class of the secondary school (Amman, 1968), pp. 237–54.

10 İbrahim Olgun, Ortaokullar ile Dengi Okullar için, Din Dersleri (Istanbul, n.d.), I, pp. 52–3; M. Barāniq (et al.), al-Tarbiya al-Dīnyya (Religious education for the first class of the secondary school) (Cairo, 1969), I, pp. 21–4.

11 Ibid., pp. 25–8, 108–15.

12 O. Carré, 'Le contenu socio-économique-politique des manuels d'enseignement religieux musulman dans l'Egypte actuelle', in: Revue des Etudes Islamiques, 38/1 (1970), p. 98.

13 Religious education for the third class of the secondary school (Cairo, 1971), pp. 81–97; A. al-Sā'iḥ (et al.), al-Tarbiya al–Dīnya (Religious education for the first class of the middle school) (Amman, 1972), pp. 11–29.

14 N. Armaner, Ilköğretmen Okulları Ders Kitalpları. Din Bilgisi (Istanbul, 1960), II, pp. 122, 143.

15 See, e.g., Religious education for the third class of the secondary school (Cairo, 1971), pp. 10ff., 58, 106ff.

16 N. Akşit, Orta Okullar için Tarih, III, pp. 215–6; F. Al-Darīnī, al-Tarbiya al-Islāmiyya (Religious education for the third class of the secondary school) (Damascus, 1971–2), pp. 236–41.

17 M. Berger, Islam in Egypt Today (Cambridge, 1970), pp. 73–84.

18 M. Okutan, Orta (2), Din Dersleri (Istanbul, n.d.), p. 38.

19 M. Barāniq (et al.), al-Tarbiya al-Dīniyya (Religious education for the second class of the secondary school) (Cairo, 1967), II, pp. 116–32.

20 Al-Manāhiǧ al-Dirāsiyya (Curricula for the secondary schools) (Amman, 1962), p. 12.

21 N. Armaner, op. cit., II, p. 35.

22 I. al-Tamīmī (et al.), al-Tarbiya al-Islāmiyya (Religious education for the second class of the middle school) (Amman, 1972), pp. 161–79; Religious education for the third class of the secondaty school (Cairo, 1971), pp. 50–1.

23 Religious education for the third class of the secondary school (Damascus, 1971–2), pp. 234–5.

24 A. al-Kayyāt, al-Tarbiya al-Dīniyya (Religious education for the third class of the secondary school) (Amman, 1973), pp. 252–3; Religious education for the second class of the middle school (Amman, 1972), pp. 177–9.

25 N.Z. Konrapa, İmam-Hatip Okolları Ders Kitapları, Peygamberimizin Hayatı (Istanbul, 1964), I, pp. 87–8.

[26] I. ᶜĀbidīn (et al.), al-Qirā'a al-Hadītha (Cairo, 1972), pp. 43–8.
[26a] See in addition O. Elwan, 'Das Problem der Empfängnisregelung und Abtreibung (Die herrschende Auffassung des Staates und der religiösen Kreise in islamischen Ländern)', in: Zeitschrift für vergl. Rechtwissenschaft, ed. O. Spiess, vol. 70, pp. 27–79; also: E. Gräf, 'Die Stellungnahme des islamischen Rechts zu Geburtenregelung (Tanzim Al-Nasl) und Geburtenbeschränkung (Tahdid Al-Nasl)', in: Der Orient in der Forschung, ed. W. Hoenerbach (Wiesbaden, 1967), pp. 210–32.
[27] Al-Ġazālī, Ihyā' ᶜUlūm al-Dīn (Cairo, A.H. 1356), IV, pp. 151–2; A. Karni, 'Changes in attitudes to birth-control in Egypt', in: Ha-Mizrah He-Ḥadash, XIII, pp. 3–4 (1976), p. 238 (Hebrew).
[28] A. Karni, op. cit., p. 239.
[29] See G.E. von Grunebaum, Islam: Essays on the Nature and Growth of a Cultural Tradition (London, 1961), pp. 127–40.
[30] See, e.g., Religious education for the third class of the secondary school (Cairo, 1971), pp. 63–84.
[31] Ibid.
[32] M. Barāniq (et al.), al-Tarbiya al-Dīnyya (Religious education for the first class of the secondary school) (Cario, 1969), I, pp. 105–6.
[33] Religious education for the third class of the secondary school (Damaskus, 1971–2), pp. 25, 26, 74, 80.
[34] Religious education for the third class of the secondary school (Cairo, 1971), pp. 98, 118.
[35] Y. al-Hamādī & M. Wahdān, al-Tarbiya al-Dīniyya al-Islāmiyya (Religious education for the sixth class of the elementary school) (Cairo, 1974), pp. 64ff.; Religious education for the third class of the secondary school (Cairo, 1971), p. 99; M. Barāniq (et al.), al-Tarbiya al-Dīnyya (Religious education for the second class of the secondary school) (Cairo, 1967), II, pp. 88–9.
[36] Ibid., p. 90; Religious education for the sixth class of the elementary school (Cairo, 1974), p. 71.
[37] Religious education of the third class of the secondary school (Cairo, 1971), pp. 125–42; for the third class of the secondary school (Amman, 1973), pp.330–1.
[38] See W.C. Smith, Islam in Modern Histroy (New York, 1959), pp. 165–207.
[39] Y. al-Ḥamādī (et al.), al-Qirā'a al-Thānawiyya li 'l-Saff al-Thālith al-Thānawi (Cairo, 1970), pp. 86f.
[40] Religious education for the first class of the middle school (Amman, 1972), pp. 172–9; Religious education for the sixth class of the elementary school (Cairo, 1974), pp. 120–1; Religious education for the third class of the secondary school (Damascus, 1971–2), p. 183; Religious education for the third class of the secondary school (Cairo, 1971), pp. 125–42.
[41] Religious education for the second class of the secondary school (Cairo, 1967), II, p. 94; the third class of the secondary school (Damascus, 1971–2), p. 162.
[42] See, e.g., ibid., pp. 46–9.
[43] Ibid., p. 36.
[44] I. al-Tamīmī et al.), al-Tarbiya al Dīniyya (Religious education for the second class of the secondary school) (Amman, 1972), p. 92.
[45] Religious education for the this class of the secondary school (Damascus, 1971–2), p. 36.
[46] See, e.g., al-Qirā' a wa'l-Maḥfūẓāt (for the sixth class of the elementary school) (Cairo, 1971), pp. 185ff.; al-Tarbiya al-Qawmiyya (Civics for the third class of the middle school) (Cairo, 1971), p. 701; Religious education for the sixth class of the elementary school (Cairo, 1974), pp. 101–8.
[47] O. Carré, op. cit., p. 124.

# Continuity and Conflict in the Monotheistic Tradition

*Hasan Askari*

## *1. Introduction*

The question of the Oneness or Unity of God can never be wholly resolved. It is a mystery *par excellence*. The conviction that God is one is present in every religion, sometimes expressly and sometimes implicitly. But every religious community always contains people who, few in number and withdrawn from the public gaze, strive in humility and awe to achieve knowledge of this divine mystery, if only for a fleeting moment. The prophets, saints and all those who were dissatisfied with the apparent finiteness of the world, followed this path. The Unity of God is a centre to which the knowledge of the visible world is drawn. But it is also the 'kaᶜba' of the revelations of hidden wisdom. Hence this Oneness of God is the light of both 'šarīᶜa' and 'tarīqa', the source of all reality and the throne of power, before which we all bow down in complete subjection. It is the principle of wisdom and of truth. The currents of all the sciences, of both the natural and the human sciences, spring from the heights of the knowledge of the unity of God, and ultimately they flow into the great ocean of His mysteries. The testimony of the one God is acknowledged by many, but investigation of it is reserved to a few. It is the easiest and the simplest question, as the masses suppose, and at the same time it is so difficult that the intellectual ability of even the greatest among the wise quavers at this problem.

Tawḥīd (oneness, being one, making one) is a judgment: that something is one, a unity. The mystics of the world of Islam define Being One in so far as its mysteries are revealed to them. Hence there are two modes of Being One: 1. The Oneness of the Law, that God of Himself is from eternity, and alive by virtue of His Life, hearing by virtue of His Hearing, seeing by virtue of His Seeing, and speaking by virtue of His Discourse. This oneness is perceptible and simple. It is perceptible by imitation of someone's example, or on the basis of rational arguments, or through faith in the principles handed down by tradition. 2. The Oneness of the Way: it is the testimony to the Oneness and Uniqueness of God in the light of everyone's own faith; it is the contemplation of God as an absolute existence, whereas all other existences cease or exist only in the Being of God. This perception of God requires neither imitation, nor argument, nor tradition.

There are several stages of the oneness of the way. Active Oneness is a condition in which all things and events are seen as activities of God. The Oneness of attributes, of characteristics, is a condition in which all attributes of all existences are perceived as attributes of God. The next is the Oneness of Absolute Self, in which all existences of all things are considered as the Existence of God. Accordingly the only real Being is that of God: there is no other. This Oneness of reality refutes all that is, including an individual self. Here all boundaries disappear, nothing remains – only authentic Being – God. One sees only God, or God sees Himself. There are several degrees of this Oneness of reality.

First there is the *Oneness of self-extinction*. By reason of the fact that God is the closest of all to human beings, God allows His light to illumine the being of the mystic, so that self-consciousness and the self of the mystic are extinguished. He (God) is with you, wherever you may be, said the voice of the Koran. In this degree of Oneness, one mystic said: 'I am sublime, and my glory is the greatest', and another said: 'I am the Truth'.[1]

Then comes the *Oneness of perception of the world.* By virtue of His Being as Light of heaven and earth, God allows His light to shine into the eyes of the mystic, who thereby sees all existence as Unity. In this state one mystic cries: 'He is All'.

The next is the *Oneness of Names*. The mystic attains to this level of Oneness by means of concentrated repetition of the Name of God, and in every name he sees the light of God, and there remains absolutely no otherness.

There is, however, still a fourth degree, and in this dimension God sends His light to illumine all the mystic's perceptions, his seeing and hearing and feeling. Then the mystic is given peace in every sensual modality afforded by the world and its changing temporalities.

In the degree of Oneness by analogy, the mystic sees every individual existence as the one Reality itself. In this state, subjection to an idol or love of a finite object or a person is an act of subjection to God. This degree of Oneness – which I have already mentioned –, in which God is seen as active in every procedure and in every action, does not however banish awareness of joy and mourning. Only in the *Oneness of perception of the world* does God bestow His light in such abundance on the mystic that the veil of darkness is finally torn aside: light upon light flood over the mystic's understanding, so that he is enveloped by non-circumstantial understanding and uninterrupted perception of all reality. Now all consciousness of joy and sadness disappears completely. The mystic, like the world of his actions, is deprived in this stage of any individual consciousness. There is no difference between perception and perceived.

The final and highest degree of *Oneness* is that of *abstraction*. On this level, the whole world of creation is extinguished in the illumination of the countless glories of the Light of God. The mystic is emptied of everything apart from the Creator. All existences and attributes are thus transcended. The world of finiteness is left behind, and a great wave breaks from the sea of being and drowns the mystic in nothingness. Thus he is born twice and extinguished twice. At this spot there is complete emptiness: it is neither earth nor heaven, neither feeling nor knowing, not even the knowledge of the Absolute. Nothing remains. There is a time with God in which no one is close to Him, neither the most trustworthy angel nor the most beloved Prophet.[2] It is a oneness of fulfilment, and also known as the primal Oneness, the divine and eternal Oneness.

Hence the mystic reaches Oneness upon Oneness. He first moves in the direction *of* God, then *with* Him, and finally *in* Him. Then he returns to the original state in the consciousness of God – nameless and undetermined. It was said of this state that there is nothing worth mentioning about it.[3] In it man is said to be engulfed in a span of time in which he has neither bodily nor spiritual existence.

To possess the two last degrees of Oneness, one is wholly dependent on the grace of God. Here no one may venture to use his understanding or powers of imagination. Hence Muḥammad's warning: Meditate on creation, not on the being of God.[4]

For every believer it is difficult to say: no God apart from God. Hence the danger of hypocrisy often arises. Righteousness in this area means that one is profoundly steeped in the knowledge that God is One through His own unity. Everything but His countenance disappears.[5]

Ǧunyad of Bagdad is said to have remarked that the knowledge of God is separate from God as being. To know God means testifying to Him. The highest point of this process is that one should oneself deny the act of testifying. Abū Bakr Wāsiṭī holds in this respect that there is no creation (ḫalq) in truth (ḥaqq), and no truth in creation. The interpretation of Oneness is to be distinguished from the reality of Oneness. The former belongs to the Prophetic stream and the latter is the sea. Where our discourse (interpretation) contains duality, our heart effaces it. When the seeker reaches the level of the heart, his tongue is maimed. When the spirit is directed towards Oneness, the heart is also reduced to silence. Then whatever is spoken, felt and done is from Him (minhu) to Him (ilayhi).

Who will dare to enter into the wilderness of God's Oneness? To affirm it is to spoil it.[6]

So long as someone, heedful of self, speaks of God, he falls into the fatal error of associating with God that which is other. So long as someone, heedful of God, speaks of himself, he strengthens his hypocrisy. Whoever maintains his being before the Being of God is lost. Whoever, expecting God, seeks his own self, knows neither. Whoever sees himself does not see God. Whoever sees God does not see himself.

The mysteries of the mystical cult are symbolic in structure. It is not Oneness itself. As aids to understanding one ought to learn the distinction between the power (qudrat) and the Oneness (waḥdat) of God. The phenomenal world enters existence out of God's power. But that phenomenal world is extinguished in His Oneness. One cannot deny the world of phenomena because that is tantamount to a denial of God's power. But one cannot affirm the phenomenal world because that is tantamount to avowal of something amiss in Oneness and of the loss of Unity. The power of God allows us to perceive ourselves and the world, whereas the Oneness of God destroys this perception – and consequently the whole phenomenal world. Death is no more than return to Oneness. It is perhaps preferable to be non-existent but with Truth than to exist in a permanently attentive state yet struggle to abstract Oneness from multiplicity.

God's Oneness for him who believes in that Oneness is a veil drawn over the sanctity of Oneness. Oneness is a miracle. Oneness comprises one's being lost in it or Its Being lost in one. Oneness is known only to the One. What is Oneness? It is one's own disappearance before the power of Unity. One should dwell with the One and not with being one. What is Oneness? It is the surrender of being one on account of Oneness. It is the transcendence of transcendence.

Bāyazid al-Bisṭāmī said once that both dominance and serfdom are represented in man. Ǧunayd of Baghdad believed that there was nothing in the body that he was accustomed to bear with him but God. Now is the moment to say: No one thinks of God but God thinks of His Self, and no one sees Him but *He* sees Himself. God is the Absolute. He is unbounded Existence, nameless and beyond all symbols and signs, free from all determining factors. All these earthly things and – above them all – the stars and the planets, all spirits, men and animals, the Torah, the Bible and the Koran, the angels and the prophets, kings and saints, all enter existence by the will of God to manifest Himself.

When all these things disappear, then this Existence which brought them into being will be as It was before any creation of any kind began. Consequently we should meditate and ask: where did all this come from, and where is it going? But: Nothing came from anywhere, nor does it go anywhere. Existence was never the other in regard to the Creator, nor is it an other, nor will it ever be an other.

It is nothing next to God. Names and signs in the world indicate: God, prophets, saints, angels, djinn, human beings, spirits, devils, heaven and earth are the ideas and myths of mankind, a fantastic product of man's incomplete understanding and his self-intoxicated imaginative power. In truth there is neither a self-prostrating being nor an object of self-prostration: neither worshipper nor worshipped; neither Adam nor Satan; there is only eternal Being, uncreated, all glorious, and unending. And no one might see Him or understand Him, for He is beyond all understanding and analogy, transcending all supposition and superstition. He is as He was and will be as He is, neither diminishment nor increase, One and Unique, Incomparable and Single.

God is neither negated by negation nor demonstrated by demonstration, nor rejoices at obedience, nor is injured by sins, nor gracious to the believer, nor diminished by the oblivious, nor closer to the wise, nor more distant from the unknowing, nor friendly to the submissive, nor inimical to the proud. He is raised above all covenants. Some of us in the power of our imaginations would manufacture idols of God. Others, more cunning, would fashion names and words of Him and pray to Him. Whether one calls Him Redeemer or Tempter, He is the same and the only God. Whence comes the other?

All religions produce images, and therefore they remain preliminary. God is one and thus raised up above everything, and His knowledge is one and in this Divine Knowledge is the world. Therefore the world is nothing other than His Knowledge. It is knowing in the Being of God, and it is the world in this knowing. It is knowing in the being of man, and in this knowing there is the knowledge of God with all His Grace and Glory. Man is in the knowledge of God and God is in the knowledge of man. God is superimposed on man and man is superimposed on God. Who is the dot and who the circumference? Who is the lord and who the slave?

## 2. *The Koran: convergence of metaphysics and sociology*

The Koran uses two terms for Deity: ilāh and allāh. The first is used eighty times in the Koran and terms derived from it sixty-nine times. The second term, allāh, is to be found in the Koran nine hundred and eighty times. Ilāh appears to stand for Deity to which man is directed either by convention or imagination. Hence ilāh is more a socio-psychological category. Allāh, on the other hand, is the only real ilāh, and a transcendental reality *par excellence*. Ilāh has a plural, ilāhin, whereas allāh has no plural. Therefore allāh is absolute Oneness. This is trans-religious, for it is universal, whereas ilah is the central requirement of religion. Therefore the Prophet tells us that allāh should not be allowed to be thought of as one of the ilāhin.

There are three kinds of Oneness or forms of being one in the Koran: one regarding ilāh: that God is One; another regarding nafs: that the self of man, as God made it, is one; and finally regarding ummat, if God had so wished it: that the human community could have been one.[7] Therefore it would seem that the Koran uses the term nafs ontologically, with reference to human being. The creation of man in the beginning, and the new creation or resurrection of man on the Day of Judgment, are similar to the creation and resurrection of a self or a person (Koran 31 : 28). On the other hand, the term ummat-i wāḥida refers to the wish that mankind should follow a religious and spiritual path. Apart from

Suras 21 : 92 and 23 : 52, where such a being one is enjoined in regard to the fear and worship of God, the Koran does not really maintain the prospect of a human community. The following Sura makes this plain: 'He could have made you one nation: but it is His wish to prove you by that which He has bestowed upon you. Vie with each other in good works, for to Allah you shall all return and He will declare to you what you have disagreed about' (5 : 48).

The Koran does appear to support the polarity of nafs and ummat, and it is the latter which constitutes human historicity. Hence the profound sociological significance of Islamic monotheism and monopsychism.

'Fellow prisoners', inquired the prophet Joseph, 'are numerous gods better than Allah, the One, the Almighty?' (12 : 39). This is the question which makes the history of monotheism so dynamic. Men find it really odd that they are summoned to invoke only one God (5 : 39). The following Sura is virtually a satire on the human situation: '... when Allah was invoked alone, you disbelieved; but when you were bidden to serve other gods beside Him you believed in them. Today judgment rests with Allah, the Most High, the Supreme One' (40 : 12).

One of the marks of Islamic monotheism is therefore its insistent recall of sirk, the phenomenon of association of false ilāhin (gods) with the true ilāh (absolute Deity). Testimony to the one God should therefore be free from all associations (4 : 19); the frequently repeated counsel not to connect anything with God (18 : 26; 18 : 38; 18 : 42; 18 : 49; 72 : 2); to worship nothing apart from God (18 : 110; 72 : 8); to fear nothing apart from God (33 : 39); and: there is no refuge apart from God (72 : 22). Hence the insistence of the Koran that 'waḥīd' (one) is also 'subḥān' (pure). It is also very significant that in the Koran belief in the *one* God is associated with belief in 'al-aḫira' (the resurrection and last judgment), and it appears that metaphysics and eschatology constitute *one* totality in Islam (39 : 45; 14 : 22). It is this oneness that provides Islam with a specific vision of society and history. The metaphysical, the eschatological and the sociological are so intimately related as to comprise one of the most mysterious and at the same time one of the most dynamic systems of thought and behaviour.

*3. The problems of the monotheistic thesis: Islamic monotheism*

It is always the institutionalized idea of God and the institutionalized ideas of fate and associated human behaviour which constitute the focal points of the historical thrust of a particular community of religious believers. Thomas O'Dea indicates certain dilemmas in the institutionalization of religion.[8] The question of monotheism is probably to be grouped among the symbolic dilemmas: objectification as against alienation. Is it true that the radical monotheism of Islam, which is opposed to any form of objectification, concurs with the other extreme of alienation? Does strict adherence to the unity of knowledge infer that God is sole ('waḥīd') and far distant ('baᶜīd') Furthermore: does the monotheistic faith of Islam on the formal canonical level (no God but God), and on the highest level of mystical consciousness (everything is God, or: God is everything), sort with its abstraction on the level of liturgy and law?

Moreoever: the metaphysics of monotheism is not easily accessible to psychological analysis. Modern psychological explanations of religion[9] do not seem to take into account one of the most significant functions of monotheism: namely, that it leads to the unicity of human experience, without which neither moral nor spiritual experience of reality is possible. The well-known notion of religion as a form of compensation for frustration does not fit the transcendental mode of the concept of oneness, whether this oneness is predicated of God or of man. It is however undeniable that modern psychological and sociological attempts to explain religious phenomena before the period of Judaism, Christianity and Islam opened up the dispute whether the religious history of mankind is unified. Therefore one should resort to the possibility that the psychological unicity of mankind, as accepted by Freudians and Jungians, has its metaphysical counterpart in the idea of the one God.[10] Here two very far-reaching questions arise: 1. Should we see the idea of the One God as no more than an evolutionary device in the course of religious development? 2. Is the idea of the One God, though constitutive in every religion, independent of religion, and therefore not a religious idea *per se*?

Hence the explanation of religion can never be an explanation of the Unity and Oneness of God. Psychology and sociology merely, so it seems, elide the metaphysics of divine Oneness.

The sociological thesis, maintained by Durkheim and his disciples, that religious categories are sociological categories *par excellence*, is equally significant. But the concept of the religious that is at the basis of this sociological formulation, namely that the religious is 'a form of speculation about everything which in general is inaccessible to science and precise thought', and that the religious is an attempt to conceive the inconceivable and to express the inexpressible, seems to rely on neglect of the fact that the monotheistic religions, though fully recognizing the Mystery which God is,[11] replace that mystery by the reconstruction of a living relationship (covenant, love, wisdom and oneness) between man and God. Hence it is also doubtful that monotheistic religion is not free from the necessity of religious legitimation, or theodicy.[12]

Radical Islamic monotheism, therefore, might well be more comprehensible against the background of some of the greater religious motifs which make up the Jewish religion and early Christian history. Only then could we understand why Islam cleaves to the Oneness of God as the resolution of many religious dilemmas. I am indebted in this respect to the reconstruction of religion in ancient history proposed by Brandon.[13]

The problems of birth, death and nourishment were the first questions to be resolved by magical-religious means. The first humans experienced the transience of things as a mysterious experience. Death was the mystery of mysteries. Ultimately, death could be looked in the face by dividing phenomena into physical and spiritual (or psychological). The idea of the soul was a conceptual victory over death. But does death return? The ancient Egyptians solved the problem by believing in the resurrection of Osiris. Another precise investigation of the objectivity of death and its implications for the significance and destiny of human life was the Babylonian Gilgamesh epic.

The greatest religious transformation, however, came about through two Hebrew ideas: that of the transcendent God and that of the judgment of the dead. The world acquired a spiritual order and a moral purpose. With the arrival of transcendentalism and eschatology, the problems of innocent suffering in regard to the idea of a just and all-powerful God and the uncertain relationship between faith and history became more prominent. Was the Christian answer a prelude to the Islamic inclusiveness of God and man? Or was the Christian answer, though adequate for the resolution of Job's paradox, reached at the cost of the transcendental aspect of God? Did Islam, by replacing God's transcendental aspect, restore the contradictions of the relationship between God and Job? Is transcendentalism right or wrong in regard to the dissolution of human suffering? Surely the concept of Oneness is better than transcendentalism? – Oneness not as a counterpart to transcendentalism but including transcendentalism and the immanent forms of consciousness of God.

The idea of Oneness could be conceived in the sense of monolatry[14] or of monotheism. The problems regarding continuity and conflict in the monotheist tradition might be framed as follows: 1. The theist notion of the One God is always in conflict with the problem of theodicy. 2. Prophetic monotheism is always in danger of becoming intellectual and priestly monolatry. 3. Transcendental monotheism is always in danger of becoming sociologically irrelevant.

### *4. Theism and theodicy*

Peter Berger, in The Social Reality of Religion,[15] remarks that every nomos is constantly erected against the danger, endemic to the human situation, of its destruction by anomistic forces. He also defines theodicy as an explanation of these phenomena in terms of religious legitimations, of any degree of theoretical exactitude. Theodicy, since it is a complex of ideas (capable of explaining suffering, evil and death in terms of self-denial, Last Judgment and life after death), should be promoted by all theisms. Theism becomes a social and cultural phenomenon through the medium of theodicy. Dependent on the relative logical order or rationality, a theodicy becomes a part of the intellectual and moral structure of a nation. Should the anomistic and the chaotic not be directed into nomos and order, the religious answer cannot be a principle of individual biography or a common history. Must, in that case, the religious response to the human situation always be equivalent to the contingent and anomistic in this situation? Naturally the fundamental secret of all theodicies is to refine a self-transcendent mode of understanding, so that on this basis a more or less developed and more or less conscious legitimation of theist belief is brought into play. But surely this transcendence is an illusion? Then theodicy would be the unending continuation of an illusion of transcendence? Only if the theist strategy is penetrated is man exposed to the total frustration which, in this context, would signify the awareness that he is incapable of being a masochist or sadist. To say that theodicy has collapsed in our civilization is to affirm that man today is fully conscious of the illusion which supported theodicean structures of thought.

The collapse of theodicy would then mean one of the following: 1. The anomistic and chaotic powers have gained the supremacy over nomos and order. 2. The legitimations advanced by theodicy – inasmuch as they are not securely grounded – succumb to meaninglessness. 3. The equilibrium between theism and theodicy has finally collapsed. The final deduction is relevant here.

This is perhaps the age of the theodicean vacuum. Does this also imply a theistic void?

As Peter Berger remarks, the age of revolutions was the most significant result of the dissolution of the Christian theodicy in the human mind. He maintains that history and human action in history became the dominant means for attempting a nomization of suffering and evil. The social theodicy of Christianity, its legitimation of social inequality, collapsed with the Christian theodicy. When the Christian interpretation of the world disappears, then the Christian legitimation of the social order cannot long survive.[16]

We might deduce two points from Berger's assertions: 1. There is in fact no theodicean vacuum. History and human concern have taken the place of God and divine redemption. A desacralized legitimation has become acceptable rather than a sacred order. 2. The cosmological theodicy and the social theodicy are mutually connected. The collapse of one is the dissolution of the other. If the explanation of the world has no ground, then the legitimation of the social cannot long survive.

Berger's remarks in fact refer directly to western civilization. Nevertheless they can be generalized in application to those developing societies in which the will and concern to change society and to confront 'suffering and evil' are certainly outside the structure of the theodicies of their religions. A major transformation is definitely under way. But does that really mean a complete surrender of the theist tendency? Or does it mean that a new theism, released from the traditional forms of theodicy, will come into being? It is nevertheless true that a theodicy is necessary which is party to the human situation. The mysterious nature of human destiny requires explanation. The explanation as such should become the basis of a new understanding of order. There are however certain characteristics of theodicean formulations, some of which would seem to have escaped Berger's scrutiny.

First, and most important, a theodicy is a human construction, whose degree of rationality differs from one religion to the other, from one aspect of a religion to another aspect of its history. Theodicy is a metaphysical and transcendental postulate which is perceptible in relation to the human situation. It is not legitimation *per se*, but the changing relation between religious faith and the historical situation, which makes a theodicean structure both functional and dynamic. Secular implications and actions can only become open to inspection on a theodicean basis.

Second, it is in the nature of all theodicies to preserve a critical attitude to historical and pragmatic reason. Here we have one of the functions of theodicy which is disappearing, for we are at the end of the era of theodicies. The beginning of a theodicy was characterized not only by the attempt to make a human situation bearable or comprehensible. Then it would be more of a transformation and replacement. There is no other way to understand the birth of the early Christian and Muslim communities. It is the dynamic and creative aspect of theodicean structures from which the faithful confronted and did not merely accept their situation.

Third, the close relationship between theism and theodicy, originating in the magico-religious aspect and becoming world-faith, was the only available means for man to overcome his situation. When, in another period of history, we have other means – structures such as technology and world-organizations – of overcoming our situation contingently and anomistically, then the close relation between theism and theodicy may not be requisite. The exhaustion of theodicy is not an exhaustion of theism, and a betrayed theodicy is not a betrayal of theism. When Jesus hung on the cross, the whole theodicy of the people of Jerusalem collapsed, but in that transformation a new theism was born. When Muḥammad refused to accept the superstition of his popular culture and attacked the gods which his people worshipped, the theodicean structure of Mecca was torn down, yet it was then that one of the most powerful religious movements was born. A theodicean vacuum is not a theistic vacuum. In our own era we are perhaps witnessing the birth and rise of a new theistic culture which does not need a developed theodicy. God becomes a trans-religious truth.

Four, polytheism is much better suited to theodicean attitudes than monotheism. The most imperceptible polytheistic tendency is that which exists where, beneath a seemingly monotheistic façade, the duality of God and man is maintained. A theodicy is essentially an explanation of all such dualities and pluralities, whether of existents or of attributes. Whoever is held fast in a theodicean form of thought finds it difficult to worship only *one* God. Hence the Koran says: 'When Allah alone is called on, you do not believe, but when some companions are ascribed to Him, you begin to believe'.

The collapse of theodicy is perhaps the most favourable moment for the birth of monotheism.

### *5. Monolatry and monotheism*

The question whether the concept of One and Supreme Deity was primordial to human nature, and whether all human groups from the most primitive to the most progressive possessed it, became a focus of attention not so long ago as the result of sharp controversy between religious apologists[17] and ethnologists. One of the advantages of this controversy was that it enabled certain conceptual clarifications to be made. The most significant of these was the distinction between monolatry and monotheism. The supporters of evolution among the ethnologists had rested upon the assumption that monotheism had developed from simple animistic and polytheistic principles. Religious ethnologists (if the term is permissible) were eager to show that monotheism could not develop from a monotheistic basis. This was either a misrepresentation of the universal and inherent belief in the One and Supreme Deity, or an arrogantly stubborn enmity towards the monotheistic mission of the Prophets. In other words: Monotheism is an essential and universal religious form of consciousness, and the prophetic mission was to manifest and articulate this. The most recent ethnological discoveries and their analyses, however, revealed some very significant aspects of the relationship between monotheism and polytheism.[18] The presence of belief in *One* Supreme Deity in simple cultures is shown to be an isolated phenomenon of thought, exercised by individual magicians, priests and people with a tendency to speculate. This isolated, individual speculation about the One, Supreme Deity is what Paul Radin calls 'monolatry'.[19] There are three observable stages in the development of monolatry: 1. Individualized awareness of the transcendental, guarded by the priest-seers. 2. As soon as this individualized awareness had to be shared by a general community, it became its opposite, namely polyatry. 3. This must necessarily occur in so far as abstraction, namely the monolatrist idea of the One, Supreme Deity, did not really correspond to the social and economic necessities of the group. The polytheistic structures of belief were suited to a magical-religious economy and culture. The ancient Graeco-Roman civilization and Hindu civilization are instances of this relationship between monolatry and polytheistic culture. The small group of Hanifites in Mecca at the time of Muḥammad's mission symbolized the monolatrist minority in the great mass of polytheistic society.

With the prophetic missions of Moses, Jesus and Muḥammad, a completely new situation came into being. It is characteristic of the prophetic breakthrough to have intended to make monolatrist belief the general profession of the people. Then there is a transition from monolatry to monotheism. This transition is an exceptional revolution in thinking, behaviour and personality. The isolated and fearful belief in the One, Supreme Deity becomes a general and open, communal and express belief in God. Prophetic transformation consists not so much in metaphysical categories as in a consideration of human beings, their views and behaviour. A Bedouin is transformed into an Abū Zar, an emotional dogmatician becomes one of the mightiest caliphs of the Muslims, a traveller becomes Paul, a poor child without support becomes ᶜAli b. Abī Tālib.

But the decisive factor is the fate of monotheistic belief in the post-Prophetic period of the development of religious tradition. The masses would seem to have professed minimal monotheism, and the task of interpretation and condification was reserved to an elite of theologians. The priest-seer of the simple culture is recalled in the theologian of the advanced religions. Monotheism once again became monolatry. Now the question is whether there is a sociology of this dialectic.

## *6. Transcendental monotheism and sociological relevance*

The foregoing raises certain questions. Monolatry would seem to have existed both before and after the prophetic witnesses of monotheism. In other words, monotheism is more inclined to be the possession of a few individuals, with the exceptions of periods when prophets arise in a specific culture. Pre-prophetic monolatry is priestly and cultic, whereas post-prophetic monolatry is intellectual. Society in general either transforms monolatry into the metaphysics of transcendentalism, or turns it into its opposite, namely polyatry. The one is a case of complete sociological irrelevance of the idea of the One God, and the other is a search for relevance by transformation into the opposite. In both cases, monotheism is shown to be a highly-dubious faith, which human societies had not yet learned to handle appropriately. Its dubiousness resides in its extremely spiritual nature and its highly-revolutionary sociological implications. I have already referred, at the beginning of this chapter, to the spiritual expression of witness to the One God. Now I shall refer summarily to its revolutionary sociological implications.

The summons to worship *One* God is also a summons to change the social order. Therefore monotheism is both a religious principle and an instrument of social reconstruction. The act of profession of faith in the One God is also an act of dispossession of property, state and religion. All social theodicies which legitimate inequality and suffering are therefore anti-monotheist. To say that there is no God apart from God is to maintain that all knowledge, power and riches feature God. This is realized if knowledge, power and riches are shared by all men and women. Shared knowledge is dispossessed knowledge, shared power is dispossessed power, and shared riches is dispossessed riches. Such extreme revolutionary implications of monotheism might be resisted by transforming it either into monolatry or into polyatry. Then society could become an autonomous whole, independent of the monotheist impulse. Hence the Koranic warning against turning Scripture into a form of poetry (the Arabic refers to all speculations and metaphysical cunning). In this sense, monotheism is freed from all theodicean necessity.

If the Koran is intent on removing any kind of širk (literary or symbolic modes of ascription of companions to God), it does so with the insight that in the last analysis the source of all širk is either a monopoly of monotheism in the hands of a few, or an unequal distribution of knowledge, power and riches.

But does a social revolution really require a monotheistic unheaval?

This is the question which should concern us above all else, for the fate of the entire human race and of its civilization depends upon it.

The question can be answered in two related ways. First, man knows of no other idea than that of the One God which could bring about a complete revolution in his self and in his relations to other people. All other totalitarian ideas, however effective, depend on human contingency. God is a non-contingent principle, and therefore He is truly transcendent and truly unifying. A secular revolution is a metaphor for a revolution, not revolution itself. Analogy is no substitute for reality. Second, a secular form of equality without monotheistic security is an equality without harmony. Equality is fully present only by means of reciprocal attachment. The latter can be achieved only by means of a common spiritual existence and destiny. The promise of a convergence of metaphysics, eschatology and sociology is the promise of an abolition of all conflicts in the monotheistic tradition.

## Notes

1 It was Manṣūr al-Ḥallāǧ who once called out: 'I am the truth: Ana l-haqq', and Abū Yazid al-Bisṭamī said: 'Subḥānī mā aᶜẓama šaʼnī'.

2 That is one of the prophetic traditions which in Arabic is as follows: 'Lī maᶜa llāhi waqtun lā yasaᶜuni fīhi malakun muqarrabun wa-lā nabīyun mursalun'.

3 Koran, Sura 76 : 1: 'Does there not pass over a man a space of time when his life is a blank?'

4 This is one of the prophetic traditions which reads as follows in Arabic: 'Tafakkarū fī ḫalqi llāh wa-lā tafakkarū fī dāti llāh'.

5 Koran, Sura 55 : 27–7: 'All who live on earth are doomed to die. But the face of your Lord will abide for ever, in all its majesty and glory'.

6 This is one of the sayings to be found in the biographies of the Muslim Sufis and which reads as follows in Arabic: 'Itbāt ut-tawḥīd fasādun fi t-tawḥed'.

7 Koranic Suras which refer to 'nafs' (self) as one: 4 : 1; 6 : 98; 7 : 189; 31 : 28; and 39 : 6.
Koranic Suras which refer to 'ummat' (community) as one: 2 : 213; 5 : 18; 10 : 19; 11 : 118; 16 : 93; 21 : 92; 23 : 52; 42 : 8; and 43 : 33.

8 Thomas O'Dea, Sociology and the Study of Religion (New York, n.d.). The five dilemmas discussed by O'Dea are: the dilemma of mixed motivation; the symbolic dilemma; reification against alienation; the dilemma of organized order; elaboration against effectiveness; the dilemma of demarcation; concrete definition against

replacement of the letter in favour of the spirit; and the dilemma of power: conversion against compulsion.

9 Michael Argyle, Religious Behaviour (London, 1968). Also S. Freud, The Future of an Illusion (London, 1928); id., Civilization and its Discontents (London, 1930). In the latter Freud develops his theory of frustration: that is, of religion as an attractive illusion offered in answer to the inadequacies of nature, the repression of real wishes, and the associated exploitation of the working classes by other sections of society; and also the paranoia-neurosis theory, according to which ritualistic religion is a cultural symptom comparable to paranoia.

10 C. Levi-Strauss, Totemism (London & Boston, 1963), pp. 1–2.

11 Koran, Sura 72 : 26: 'He alone has knowledge of what is hidden. His secrets He reveals to none'.

12 P. L. Berger, The Social Reality of Religion (London, 1969), pp. 53–80.

13 S. G. F. Brandon, Religion in Ancient History (London, 1973).

14 P. Radin, Primitive Religion (New York, 1957), pp. 254–67.

15 P. L. Berger, The Social Reality of Religion, op. cit., p. 53.

16 Ibid., pp. 79–80.

17 W. Schmidt & H. Binard de la Boullaye.

18 P. Radin, Primitive Religion, p. 266.

# The Prophetic Function of Faith in Contemporary Christianity

*Wilhelm Dantine*

1. Throughout its history Christian faith has continually shown itself aware of its prophetic function, in differing forms and to varying degrees, through the Church as well as through individuals and small groups. Nevertheless it can easily be established that this function has never been seriously discussed or theologically verified in the general theology of the Catholic, Orthodox and Protestant Churches. Its fate is shared in a curious way by that of theological pneumatology which, though it possesses its own theologoumena and even its own dogmas (at the latest since 362, the Synod of Alexandria), in fact neglects its prophetic elements.

Hence it is essential to name at least a few of the causes behind this historical fact.

(i) Even in the post-apostolic period the few traces of an independent prophetic ecclesial existence vanish, although there had clearly been one in the primitive Church. The prophetic office of teaching and proclamation was *de facto* absorbed into the doctrinal authority of the bishops in a relatively brief process. Christian prophecy fades into the ecclesiastical 'underground', as is demonstrated by the exemplary history of Montanism. This ecclesial underground remains the home of the prophets and this situation repeats itself, again in typical fashion, during the Reformation period, i.e. in post-Reformation Protestantism. It is interesting to note that even when a new ecclesiasticism comes into being as a result of prophetic initiative, the same sort of oppression again forces it underground, as is attested by the history of the 'radical' Reformation.

(ii) The history of 'fides quae creditur' clearly demonstrates the dogmatic basis for this development. – Of course I cannot do more than examine a few of the most important points here.

(a) Christological dogma becomes the determining factor. The rejection of the title 'prophet' for Jesus Christ, and the rejection of Jewish, Judeo-Christian and later Islamic interpretations of Christ that this implies, lead to the loss of Christ's prophetic function. In the theology of the primitive Church it still appears occasionally (Eusebius of Caesarea) alongside his functions as priest and king, but gradually vanishes in favour of the latter.

Only with the rediscovered supremacy of the 'viva vox evangelii' in the Reformation do we find a 'munus propheticum Christi' (Calvin). It was first developed by Calvinist theologians, and soon after taken up by the Lutherans, later by Catholic theology and occasionally even by some Eastern Orthodox theologies. However, even in Protestantism, in keeping with the above-mentioned suppression of any prophetic function in the Church, the Christological 'munus propheticum' is also confined to Christ as the absolute bearer of Revelation. This means that the figure of the prophet is fused with that of the proclaimer of the Word of God, represented by Christ in person: he himself becomes his own messenger.

(b) Attention should also be drawn to a particularly characteristic effect of theological development in which all the Christian Churches were and are equally involved. Early in the history of theology 'futuristic eschatology' or 'ultimate eschatology' established its absolute predominance in the doctrine of the 'last things' (*De novissimis*). The period of the 'history' between the Ascension and the Last Judgment is thus by definition excluded from any prophetic *diakonia*, since the prophetic function can only apply to the coming of the future kingdom of God which lies beyond history. The responsibility towards the future, i.e., the period preceding the dawning of perfection, which is peculiar to Old Testament prophecy, is thereby excluded, as is the certainty anchored in the proclamations of both Jesus and the Apostles that the 'kingdom' is already present here and now; this necessarily leads to neglect of the 'prophetic' function of faith. It should also be noted that the 'doctrine of divine providence' covers the period of future history. Due to the two basic concepts from which it derives, and by which it has to a varying degree been influenced, namely 'predestination' and 'sustaining grace' (*Conservatio*), it has an intrinsic tendency to exclude the prophetic functions. Both the strictness of unchangeable decisions incorporated into an ordered system and the dominance of a presupposed 'established order' forbid mobility in understanding and structuring history. Both these factors encourage the passive acceptance of the prescribed passage of history, and thus a fatalistic approach.

(iii) I shall consider once more the dogmatic development of the so-called 'fides qua creditur', in short 'pneumatology', the 'opus Spiritus Sancti', for further confirmation of the above findings.

(a) Even the dogmatic assertion of the 'pneuma hagion' in the teaching of the Fathers describes its essential function as the vital relationship between the Father and the Son: in other words, the mutual love that exists between them. For this reason, the chief function of spirituality among men remains to effect man's relationship (*religio*) to the Father as the 'fons deitatis'. Hence the Spirit simultaneously helps to glorify and strengthen the relationship to Christ, which appeared to be already established christologically. Although the 'filioque' clause dividing eastern from western Christianity places differing emphases here and there, with fundamental consequences, it does very little to alter the universally strong link between the official function of the 'pneuma' and the closed dogmatic system represented by the first two Persons of the Trinity. The 'Spirit' has the task of mobilizing faith in the Father and the Son, not of acting in his own right! This is apparent, although in a somewhat different form, in the Orthodox doctrine of theiosis, as also in the Roman doctrine of grace and in the Protestant doctrine of 'gratia applicatrix', or the 'ordo salutis'.

(b) I must also draw special attention to one of the fundamental characteristics of ecclesiastical pneumatology which was and still is capable of retarding the prophetic function of faith quite effectively. What I have in mind is the above-mentioned (and, as is acknowledged, philosophically false) understanding of *religio* as 'reference back' to the 'origin', which is essentially derived from a particular form of metaphysical source-hunting. One is almost tempted to discern in general official ecclesiastical pneumatology something like an unintentional (but always actually effective) denial of the Incarnation. I do not mean 'Incarnation' exclusively as the interpretation of a *logos* Christology, but as a summary term for God's becoming man, for God's turning to the world and self-identification with human beings in their world, so that He was put on the cross and died. The 'spirit' of this pneumatology does not extend that application to the world, and hardly even sends those affected by it into the world and its future; instead it removes them from the world and allows them to emigrate to the super-world: to super-nature, and to a metaphysical origin. Ultimately, the gnostic 're-ascent of the soul' is the basic model *behind* all these pneumatological concepts, even though it is of course renounced verbally. This is also true of the *theiosis* notion of oriental Christianity and the western theology of grace; admittedly, the Reformed doctrine of justification had a wholly different intention, but its later encounter with the *ordo salutis* made it functionally equivalent to the very return I have just spoken of.

I shall now refer to two characteristic results of this pneumatological model: they will recur in my positive treatment of this complex of problems. First, it is a matter of the gnoseological area in which every advance (not 'progress') stagnated on account of that basic pneumatological concept. On that basis it proved possible to accommodate the particular spirit of the age, but unfortunately that meant always just keeping up with it. A revolutionary advance, a prophetic break-through which would be able to see and understand the God of Abraham, Isaac and Jacob in a new light (the sort of thing that the prophets, Jesus himself, but also Paul and John, or Augustine, Thomas or Luther dared to do), presupposes a liberation of pneumatology which is certainly its prophetic mission. A second result is to be expected for the practice of faith: the above-mentioned pneumatological model is able to conceive 'rebirth' and 'sanctification' only as religious perfectionism on a moralistic level. Ultimately, Christian activity in this regard has an egotistical salvific function as a form of consolidation of the individual religious, moral and glorified existence. Mission to the world, vocation as salt of the earth and light of the world, and responsible assumption of the destiny of the world, require for their part a prophetic awareness of vocation which has to be re-established.

2. Until now I have intentionally avoided any more precise description of what exactly 'prophetic function' might mean; not only because 'the prophetic' of its very nature cannot be defined more exactly, but because first of all, its historical inadequacy

within official Christianity ought to be seen so to speak as a 'negative image', in order to show the loss suffered by Christianity through the suppression of one of its essential elements.

At this point, however, all that is possible is to offer not an overall definition, but only some elementary criteria for the prophetic; extensions and more profound details can of course be added (as, for example, in F. Mussner's contribution in the present volume).

– A prophet is characterized by direct perception of the word of God. He takes his stand on the call of God addressed to him, but only his unconditional obedience specifically characterizes him as a prophet. This obedience should not be confused with the obedience of a lower military rank, nor is it pig-headed observance of rules and prescriptions, nor the reaction of a serf, but free and autonomous response to the convincing truth of the summoning Voice, a response made out of dedication to His shaping will.

Therefore the prophet is not someone depersonalized or dehumanized to the level of a talking and moving robot, as for instance was the case of the Hellenistic mantics (cf. the *pneuma mantikon*). Nor does the prophet walk blinkered through the events of his own times. On the contrary his own age is much clearer to him, since what he hears is passed through the filter of what he himself (with attentive ears and eyes) takes from his own epoch. For the One who speaks to him, the God of Abraham, Isaac and Jacob, is the God of history who in this his own history seeks and turns to mankind.

– A prophet accepts the call of God and understands himself to be the 'mouth' of God. He becomes the one who reveals the One who reveals Himself to him. What is revealed to the prophet may in fact be but a fragment of the entire wisdom of God, but what is said to him must become perceptible through him. Therefore the prophet is an unusually uncompromising vehicle: he can and must keep nothing quiet. He is sent to open his mouth. He has to raise his voice. It is not his concern whether his listeners understand what he says or act upon it. Some might call that a reckless or disinterested attitude, but it is part of the prophetic calling to show unconditional respect for truth.

– The prophet does not, however, proclaim eternal truths which are expressed in the same way in all times and places, but truths which are highly practical and have to do with the historical circumstances of his listeners. And he never ignores in the process the whole frame of reference of time and space. For instance, the Old Testament prophets addressed their prophecies to the people of Israel, as their proverbial sayings show, but their sights were always raised, too, to the universal society of the world and mankind. This appropriateness of prophetic discourse to the historical situation fits the here-and-now of a specific historical situation but always features the tendency to reveal the lines of the future in that historical moment. The One who summons is always the Lord who is to come. Therefore prophecy is neither 'prophesying' in the popular sense, nor oracular statements about times to come, nor soothsaying, but always the disclosure of a new dimension of historical existence for today and for tomorrow.

– Prophetic discourse is therefore always a summons to human action in the sense of a total faith-experiment. This may be oriented to a wholly inward, apparently only spiritual activity (for instance, coming to terms with a guilty past by means of contrition and penance), yet such conversion transforms both man and his whole situation. Prophecy requires renewal and is therefore always promise and a summons to break out into renewal – even though in a context of apparent threat. Prophecy requires human change and innovation, as well as transformation and renewal of human conditions; transformation and renewal not only of souls, but of all historical existence which is affected thereby.

(i) What is the implication for Christology of this definition of the nature of the prophetic? This question cannot be avoided, although everyone will realize that he cannot expect an exposition of the contemporary, very lively Christological situation *in toto*. But since Christology is the innermost core of Christian belief, I must make a few important remarks in this regard.

(a) If we prescind from the above-mentioned criteria, it is immediately obvious that they to all intents and purposes reveal the image of the man Jesus of Nazareth as an historical figure. It is by no means an accident of history that the term 'prophet' was spontaneously attached to the Nazarene in his own lifetime. Not merely the Israelite-Jewish environment ordained that, or the demonstrable fact that Jesus publicly and consciously allied himself with the Old Testament prophetic tradition: it was the very nature of his person and his appearance that declared itself thus. His ear was placed as it were to the mouth of God, whose mouth he claimed to be by proxy – yet autonomous proxy. He revealed the future of mankind in the midst of his preaching of the kingdom to come, for that kingdom was something of the future as well as something already present in his own activity. That future is not, however, a fate which is to come, but a turning-point which is already present, which, by means of penance and following on the road of self-fulfilling love, places the faithful in a new dimension of relationship with God as well as of common human responsibility.

It was in this sense that the disciples, apostles and first Christian communities understood Jesus, and therefore called him the 'Anointed', the 'Lord', the 'Christ': which for them meant 'anointing of the Spirit'. Therefore he was also the 'Prophet'.

(b) I have already mentioned the controversy about the Christological concept which, while strictly preserving the Christian *credo*, is directed to the *vere deus et vere homo* question in order to ensure that the historical Jesus is no longer – as has happened for the most part hitherto – lost to view in the general abstract formula of his 'human nature'. It should be a hopeful sign that an attempt to bring Jesus the pneumatic back into human awareness might indeed be successful. The nervousness about Jesus the pneumatic and prophet which stems from the early Christological disputes, and has been virulent in church circles until the present day, is now banished by the profound insight that God manifested his presence in this very historical individual, in this actual human being. The cross to which Jesus of Nazareth was nailed precisely on account of his prophetic behaviour, should no longer be viewed with religious embarrassment as a mere point of transition – to be passed by hastily on the way to the Resurrection, as though the old order were just put back again as it was. Nor should we see the cross as the sole ending and apex: for instance, as in the widespread understanding of it as some kind of soteriological conclusion in which reconciliation and the forgiveness of sins can be as it were parcelled up as an impersonal gift for distribution to people for mere acceptance. Rather the resurrection of the Son by the Father in the Holy Spirit means a fundamental, actual confirmation by God of the pneumatic Prophet Jesus; which also means, however, a ratification and legitimation of his word and his actions right up to his death abandoned by God: the death by which this one man demonstrated his absolute solidarity with humankind, including the thieves on the cross.

(c) In this perspective the formula 'cross and resurrection' is saved from descent to the status of an empty if pious formula – if, that is, the liberating action of the historical Jesus becomes the assurance of a universal humane 'liberation', and therefore an affirmation that the spark of the Spirit ignites a process of liberation based upon the reconciliation of personal and social guilt. The 'spiritual event' in the sacrifice on the cross (cf. Heb. 9 : 14) makes possible, motivates and impels the sacrifice of the faithful in rational service of God (Rom. 12 : 1). We might also say that Christology leads directly to pneumatology.

(ii) The above-mentioned inward correlation between Christology and pneumatology is also ultimately the key to the connection between historicity and prophecy. The traditional models of the *fides* doctrine make drastically clear how very far they are from the early Christian notion of anointing by the Spirit; even the Protestant version with the triad of *notitia-assensus-fiducia* is no exception, but merely serves to confirm the loss of the prophetic dimension. This is apparent too in the atrophying of the theologoumena 'vocation' and 'illumination', but also sanctification. These notions are, however, capable of affording a new approach: they define the gnoseological problem involved, and the historical field of action where faith must prove itself in practice, to which I have referred above.

(a) The history of the German translation of *illuminatio*, 'illumination', may serve to illustrate the fate of the doctrine of the Spirit. *Erleuchtung* (enlightenment) became the favoured term of a variety of Pietism which bowed unquestioningly to the dictates of a biblicist dogma, condemned all gnoseological questions as the work of the devil, and was interested exclusively in the psycho-volitional impulsions of the heart. The term *Erweckung* (awakening) so to speak escalated this particular tendency of interpretation of illumination. In contradistinction to this movement, the *Aufklärung* (the German Enlightenment) was the accepted term for a way of understanding the world and oneself which saw itself as secular, even though it did not understand the autonomy of human thought and action as in principle opposed to Christian belief, but did see that independence as the *conditio sine qua non* of a gnoseological process. This basic tendency was to all intents and purposes 'historicized' by German idealism and romanticism as far as its understanding of Spirit was concerned.

The confrontation between pious 'illumination' (*Erweckung*) and secular 'Enlightenment' (*Aufklärung*) shows that the Enlightenment offered a kind of wholly autonomous, and therefore secularized, prophetism, whereas the pious movement reduced prophetism to a minimum. But illumination by the Holy Spirit means both: the pious movement of the heart *and* the independent and autonomous claim to be oneself a 'mouth' of God, in order to articulate the 'Word' appropriately. This kind of illumination is founded on vocation, on God's summons, which alone first opens up the way of enlightenment, allowing the Gospel and Word of God precedence in the process of initiation into the gnoseological process, but assuring the Gospel a canonical, i.e. controlling function. Just as clearly, the 'Spirit' frees the individual, and at the same time entitles him or her to an independent liberty of understanding and individual pronouncement.

Fundamentally, this was how Christianity proceeded at the start. The so-called Hellenization and Romanization of Christianity would never have taken place, if the first theologians had not dared on their own responsibility to teach the Gospel they had received in a newly-articulated form. Whatever meaning one attributes to these key-terms, and however one may judge it, this was a decisive presupposition for the development of Christian faith as an historically effective truth. The gnoseological situation, however, would become problematical if this new incarnation of the Word of God were identified with the nimbus of an a-historical, undying and static form of truth, and the epigones were commanded to remain faithful to this first fruit of the reception of the Gospel. For so-called 'tradition' set an obstacle at the centre, one which threatened to prevent any new incarnation of the Word of God. Western and eastern church orthodoxies, as well as Protestantism (wholehartedly the same in this respect, in spite of its theoretically inimical attitude to tradition), enthusiastically competed to offer a stable form of truth that had once been historical and up-to-date, but would suffice for all epochs. This kind of 'tradition' was even celebrated as the work of the Holy Spirit. Analogously, Protestantism invoked the theory of verbal inspiration, and tried to establish the Bible as a kind of 'paper Pope'. Nevertheless there is no doubt that this kind of institutionalized spirit directly contradicts the prophetic Spirit; the forcing aside of the Spirit into secularism was only one consequence of this process.

This is not the place to discuss more closely the historical degeneration of the prophetic Spirit. But the postulate of its restoration for the gnoseological process is something that cannot be ignored. The dissolution of a static metaphysics by historical thought should be an opportunity to restore the direct hearing and irreplacable autonomy of intellectual experience, so that the Christian is once again entitled to prophetic independence in shaping and forming the truth he or she has heard. To be sure, among other things that implies a vast programme of work for contemporary theologians. The relationship of theology to philosophy, but also to the other religions, is urgently in need of reorientation – which should not be misinterpreted as mere adaptation to contemporary problems and their side-issues. What is above all important at this stage is the insight that there can be no genuine renewal of Christian faith unless the Spirit of prophecy reappears on the gnoseological level, and is fully entitled to do so.

(

(b) The prophetic dimension of the operation of faith on the realm of historical action has perhaps become more familiar to Christians today than that in the field of gnoseology. Many individual Christians, lay-people and theologians, but also church groups and committees, even authorities, have become conscious of and put into practice a certain prophetic rôle. I cannot go into specific questions here, but we certainly ought to ask what fundamental judgment we should pass on such an enterprise. In short, what has 'sanctification' to do with historical action on a socio-political level? I shall close my remarks with a concise attempt at an answer to this question.

– In so far as the Church sees itself as the 'pilgrim people of God' – and only thus does it escape the temptation of its own 'Baalization' – it accompanies all humanity on its way to its historical goal, which faith sees as the coming of the 'kingdom'. This kind of accompaniment (or *concursus,* which is Karl Barth's ingenious translation of the term) cannot be some kind of nonchalant or stolid trotting along side-by-side, nor can it be any kind of attempt to take over the rôle of universal astrologer. Instead it must be the perception of a prophetic office, which in the assurance of eschatological 'salvation' realizes its responsibility for the well-being of human society. – There is not enough space here for me to examine the complex problem of what exactly is meant here by 'Church'.

– This hope in the kingdom is founded on the experience of the action of God in Christ, through which he showed on the cross his solidarity with mankind and their involvement in guilt and death. The resurrection of Jesus confirms the openness of the future (beyond all human deaths to come) to the fulfilment of creation, to 'a new heaven and a new earth, in which righteousness reigns' (2 Pet. 3 : 13). All this substance of faith (which I have only indicated fragmentarily) may be summarized in the simple statement: 'God is love'.

– The realization of this faith is to be understood as the 'advocacy of the Spirit' and may also be seen as the prophetic office of Christians bestowed upon them by Christ. This office has a double function: One of its aspects is to be imparted and received in the direct transmission of the Gospel; all men and women are summoned to trust the word of this love: to place their lives under the sign of a love that overcomes even death.

The other function is motivated by exactly the same love, but refers to the way to be taken by mankind into the history of the future, which is still to be unfolded. Independently of individual conversion and the faith of individuals, Christian hope contributes to the 'well-being' of society and of the individual. Christian hope, however, has learnt that hope in the missionary conversion of mankind, or in its Christianization, was a false kind of utopianism. Like all forms of Christian theocracy (Christocracy), it was not only impossible but perverted. Nevertheless, and on the contrary, Christians can never cease hoping and must never stop loving. Hence their prophetic accompaniment of human history is realized in the service of love. This love, however, is not restricted to necessary and mandatory charitable assistance. It extends beyond that to participation in all the concerns proper to society. Christian social ethics would be an inclusive term for this prophetic service.

Here the circle has closed, for with this postulate we have returned to the area of gnoseological problems. We might add, however: Why should it not be Christians who go among the prophets? They are impelled by the assurance of the fulfilment of creation – they can dispense with illusionary utopias. Perhaps, however, in faith, hope and love they can project 'real utopias' for the near and distant future history of humanity, in order to provide guidelines for a responsible society. For that purpose, they need the help of the reason, knowledge and imagination of all mankind.

There is also no reason whatsoever why, in their prophetic service, they should dispense with the critical cooperation of other religions, especially the prophetic elements in Judaism and Islam.

# Africa's Contribution to the Universalism of the Bible and the Koran

*Engelbert Mveng*

The political situation prevailing today in many African countries stresses the revival of our traditional and cultural heritage. The main question is a question of *authenticity*, of cultural *identity*. We reject the colonial system as destructive of our personality. Because the Christian missions were closely connected with colonial powers, Christianity is considered as part of the colonial system: hence the question of the relevance of Christianity for Africa.

This is a very fundamental question. It also concerns Islam, another external religion, introduced to Africa by invaders and Muslim missionaries from Arabia. It has to do with the universality of these religions and their relevance for Africa.

Is the Bible only a religious and cultural heritage of the Jewish people? Does it belong exclusively to the Jewish people? Is Christianity an exclusive attribute of western civilization? Similar questions have to be posed in regard to the Koran.

Are other peoples, other civilizations, concerned with these religions? Is Africa, and Black Africa, really concerned with them? Such are the questions, and these questions are extremely important to us.

## *1. The Bible and Black Africa*

Many books, of course, have been published on the connections between the Bible and the ancient middle-eastern civilizations, including Egypt. But in these publications Egypt is not considered to be an authentic part of Africa, particularly of Black Africa.

Since the publication of some outstanding books by African scholars,[1] it has become increasingly evident that Black Africa was the cradle of the Egyptian civilization.

By Black Africa, I mean Cush, which includes Nubia, Meroe, Ethiopia, several Black kingdoms along the upper Nile valley, and some others on the eastern coast, and in the heart of the Black continent. In the Septuagint Cush was translated as Ethiopia, and Cushites as Ethiopians.

All the peoples of the Mediterranean area during this period considered Cush to be a wonderland, the country of the most religious and most beautiful people in the world. As far as the Egyptians themselves were concerned, Egypt was founded by Black dynasties (Ist to VIth dynasties), and Black dynasties restored Egypt (XXth to XXVth dynasties).

The historical situation of the people of the Bible, who lived for four hundred years in Egypt, under Egyptian domination, necessarily supposed that the Egyptian civilization influenced the evolution of the Jewish people. This is true even of their reaction against their oppressors.

If Black Africa is the cradle of Egypt, and if the people of the Bible spent so many centuries in Egypt, we have to ask what links there might be between Black Africa and the Bible.

### *2. The Congress of Jerusalem*

From April 24–27, 1972, the Panafrican Movement of Christian Intellectuals organized a congress on *The Bible and Black Africa* at the Hebrew University of Jerusalem. There were some fifty African participants from seventeen African countries, both Christians and Muslims.

At the end of the congress, they passed two main resolutions: First, they decided to found an African Institute of Biblical Studies in Jerusalem. Second, they agreed on the theme of their next congress: *The Holy Koran and Black Africa.*

Some might be surprised at the unanimity of the African participants in the congress, and the emphasis put on the sources of the three main revealed religions in the world: Judaism, Christianity and Islam.

The real reason is that all these religions are deeply rooted in the religious tradition of Black Africa. Common opinion says that Judaism, through Moses, originated from Egypt; Christianity from Judaism; and Islam from both Judaism and Christianity. During our congress at Jerusalem University, we discovered that, if the Law of Moses has an African origin, it is rooted in the religious tradition of Cush (which means Black Africa).

We all know that Moses was married to a Black woman (Num. 12 : 1ff). This woman was selected by the Lord Himself to become, spiritually and ethnically, the ancestor of the people of God. In the biographies of Moses, we read that, according to Jewish traditions, Moses, before the liberation of his people from Egypt, was received by the King of Cush, and trained in Cushite religious traditions.[2]

But what is the religious meaning of the marriage of Moses to a Black woman, in the context of his religious vocation? In the Old Testament, to marry a woman means to accept, or adopt, her social and religious traditions. That is why marriage to Midianite women was prohibited (Num. 25). That also is why God obliged Moses to repudiate Sephora, the daughter of Jethro the Midianite Priest (Ex. 28 : 1–12).

On the contrary, for Moses to choose a Black woman meant to chose a people whose religious traditions accorded with the revelation of the Bible. The real question, therefore, is the religious meaning of the marriage of Moses which, according to Philo of Alexandria, is the symbol of the election of Moses, with the privileges and graces of his vocation: 'The most glorious title of Moses is his marriage to a Black woman; this Black woman is like a precious stone, incorruptible and purified by the fire. Just as the pupil of the eye, which has the capacity of sight, is black, so we call black that part of the soul which plays the rôle of the organ of perception'.[3]

The religious meaning of this Black woman is the vocation of the non-Jewish peoples to be associated, from the very beginning, with the same Covenant which constitutes the people of God. According to Philo, this association gives the eye of revelation its spiritual dimension.

Revelation, therefore, *is not racial election*. It passes from one people to all peoples all over the world. Origen identifies this Black woman with the image of the Church which, from the darkness of the various pagan peoples, came to the light of true faith and became the bride of Christ: 'Indeed, says the Church, I am the Black wife of Moses. I am Black because of my origin; I am beautiful because of my conversion and my faith'.[4] This symbolism, in the Old Testament, concerns not only the wife of Moses, but the Black people of Cush, as a people.

The notion of a people is very important in the Old Testament. Therefore we must remember that, through the election of the people of the Bible, God reveals the election of the people of Cush, which is the symbol of the election of non-Jewish peoples. Ebed-Melech, the black servant of King Zedekiah, saves Jeremiah the prophet from the cistern. Then God makes a *perpetual covenant* of peace and salvation with Ebed-Melech, for himself and for his descendants. (Jer. 38 : 7ff).

Phinehas, the Black man, is a grandson of Aaron. His mother is Puthiel, a Black woman from Egypt. He is chosen by God to exterminate those who have married pagan women from Midian, mixing the pagan traditions of these women with the holy tradition of the people of the Covenant. Phinehas appears here as the protector of the people of God from any religious contamination with paganism. After the mission of Phinehas, the Lord concludes: 'I make with him a covenant of peace, for him and for his posterity, a covenant of *perpetual priesthood*, because of his commitment to the service of God! (Num. 25 : 12–3).

In Isaiah we read concerning the people of Cush: 'In those days, offerings will be brought to the Lord Sabaoth by the indomitable and powerful people of Cush' (Is. 18 : 5–7). And the prophet Zephaniah says: 'From beyond the rivers of Cush, my worshippers, my dispersed sons, will bring me their offerings' (Zeph. 3 : 10). The Psalmist adds: 'The people of Cush will raise its hands to the Lord Sabaoth'.

The Queen of Sheba, according to a common tradition, was Cushite, and she became, with King Solomon, the ancestor of the dynasty of Axum. This corresponds exactly to the rôle of Moses, who became, with his Black wife, the spiritual ancestor of the people of God. It reminds us of the Song of Songs: 'Black I am and beautiful... The King therefore loved me and introduced me into his palace' (Can. 1 : 4–5).

Through all these passages, we discover that the favour of the Lord is given indeed to Black individuals, but also to the Black people as a people.

The Black people are not considered here because of their power or richness, but as a religious people: 'From beyond the rivers of Cush, my worshippers, my dispersed sons, will bring me their offerings' (Zeph. 3 : 10). This opinion is confirmed by many sources external to the Bible. We read in Diodorus of Sicily: 'They say that the Ethiopians were the first to be taught to honour the gods and to hold sacrifices and processions and festivals, and the other rites by which men honour the Deity; and that in consequence their piety has been published abroad among all men, and it is generally held that the sacrifices practised among the Ethiopians are those which are the most pleasing to heaven...'[5]

To confirm this opinion, Diodorus calls upon Homer, 'the oldest and certainly the most venerated among the Greeks, who, in the Iliad, wrote:

> ... Zeus has yesterday to Ocean's bounds
> Set forth to feast with Ethiop's faultless men
> And he was followed there by all the gods.[6]

After this quotation, Diodorus adds: 'And they state that, by reason of their piety towards the deity, the Ehiopians manifestly enjoy the favour of the gods...'[7]

Even in the literature of the non-Jewish peoples of those times, the Black people were considered principally as a religious people.

It is not astonishing, therefore, if we find Black communities converted to Judaism long before the Christian era. The modern Fellasha of Ethiopia continue this very old tradition.

When we consider the religious significance of the rôle of Cush throughout the Old Testament, we are not surprised to discover that one of the first non-Jewish people to be converted to Christianity was a Black pilgrim from Cush, a minister of Candace, Queen of the Ethiopians (Acts 8). This conversion symbolizes the accomplishment of the Old Testament in the New Testament. St John Chrysostom, commenting on this 'Black' passage, shows that the conversion of this Black pilgrim is a perfect model of Christian conversion, which is an attitude of total faith before the Lord, without asking for signs or miracles: 'The Apostles followed the Lord, saw the miracles and believed; St Paul on his road to Damascus heard a voice and the thunder from heaven, and he believed. This Black pilgrim saw no miracle, heard no voice, and he believed!'[8]

Of course, we are not concerned with the modern, political Messianism of the Black Jews from the USA. Our interest is in the religious meaning of the notion of the *people of God*. The people of God does not depend upon the fact that one is ethnically Jewish. The wife of Moses was not Jewish. Puthiel, the mother of Phinehas, was not Jewish. But by the testament of

God given to them, they created a new people, the people of God, multiracial but one family in one faith.

The notion of *people* in the Bible, therefore, is firmly connected with the *universality* of the message of God. This is connected with the universality of the election of all peoples as people of God. The biblical message is addressed to all men of all nations all over the world, and it is part of the spiritual heritage of all men all over the world. For us Africans, there are historical, anthropological, cultural and religious grounds to show that the Bible belongs to our spiritual and traditional heritage; and its message speaks to our peoples in their own languages. There is, therefore, an African way of reading the Bible. The message of the Bible, addressed to African peoples, needs an African reply, which cannot be given by another people. We have to read the Bible with our own eyes, to listen to the voice of the Lord with our own ears, to answer Him with our own voice. Nobody can replace us in this historical task. What we say for the Bible is also true for the Koran. Since we have not yet held the congress on the Koran and Black Africa, we cannot yet fully describe the historical and religious links between Black Africa and the sources of the Koran. We know that there were Black people among the first companions of the Prophet. Some were leaders of prayer, dancers and musicians like Billal, the famous Black companion of Muḥammad.

From the very beginning, the people of Allah was founded on faith, not on any racial discrimination. For Africans, to be converted to Islam is to become a member of the people of believers, to enter the family of faith.

It would be very interesting to study the traditions of origin among the Muslim communities of Black Africa. They very often affirm that they received their faith from Ukba their ancestor, who was a disciple of Muḥammad and a companion of Omar. Ukba is their ancestor both spiritually and ethnically. This tradition means that, for Africans, all believers are but one family, but this family is not composed of one race, one people or one nation. It is multiracial and universal. The second meaning of this legend is that the Holy Koran belongs to the spiritual heritage of all members of the family of Islam. There is therefore an African way of reading the Koran, and nobody can replace Africa in this task. That is why, in West Africa, the elite speak of Negritude and Islam.

I am aware of the questions behind these very difficult problems. To speak of an African way of experiencing the biblical message supposes a deep and constant familiarity with the Bible and its historical and religious background. The same is true of the Holy Koran. The problem is not merely a question of religious nationalism. What we need today in Africa is people of faith and people of the Holy Scripture. To live the message of the scriptures more authentically, more Africanly, is to make this message more universal.

When we speak of an African way concerning the Bible, we do not mean any monopoly over the Bible. We only mean the original contribution of Africa to the universality of the message of the Bible. Without African peoples, the people of God cannot be universal. Without African contribution, the message of God is not universally expressed, received and accomplished. The time has come for Africa to make its contribution to the edification of the people of God.

This is a major project. It needs time, men and institutions. The resolution of the Jerusalem Congress on the Bible and Black Africa is a consequence of this evidence.

We appeal to all individuals, communities, religious agencies, private or public foundations, to help us found at Jerusalem an *Institute of Biblical Studies for Africans.*[9]

## Notes

1 Cheikh Antiadiop, De l'anteriorité des civilisations négro-africaines, mythe ou réalité historique (Paris, 1967); Theophile Obenga, L'Afrique dans l'Antiquité: l'Afrique Noire et l'Egypte pharaonique (Paris, 1972).

2 See Philo of Alexandria, De Vita Mosis; Flavius Joseph, Contra Apionem; id., Antiquitates Judaicae, lib. I, x, 238ff. See also the many sources quoted by Eusebius of Caesarea in his Praeparatio Evangelica (PG, XXI, 729ff.)

3 Comment. Alleg., lib. I, xviii, 67.

4 Origen, Cant. PG XIII, 104–6.

5 Lib., III, ii, 1–4.

6 Iliad, I, 423–4.

7 Lib. III, ii, 1–4.

8 Hom. XIX in Act. Apost., PG LX, 154 : 4.

9 The African Ecumenical Centre in Jerusalem has now been established. It was inaugurated on 10 August 1980 at St Anna's White Fathers' House, Old City, Jerusalem, under the auspices of the Ecumenical Association of African Theologians.

# The Universal Responsibility of the Revealed Religions

*Richard Friedli*

The religions are inconceivable without any reference to the world, but this mundane relevance is different in each case. The prophetic type of religion conceives the world and its history as the location for the realization and penetration of the Word of God. Therefore the world has to be accepted as a responsibility. In the so-called mystical religions, on the other hand, the world is associated with the circumambient suffering of all creatures; then salvation is apparent for the seeker after redemption only in flight from the world, and the world is evaluated negatively.

This phenomenological typology of religions cannot be equated with historical religions. That would be an intolerable simplification of their nature. Orientation to and contempt for the world are rather tendencies which are to be found in every so-called major religion. Accordingly it is somewhat inexact to speak of revealed religions (as distinct from the mystical religions and mythical tribal religions). Only when speaking in such inexact and general terms is it possible to discuss the universal reference of the revealed religions.[1] Acceptance of the world is to be found also in Hinduism (one thinks in this regard of Gandism) and in Buddhism (there is the school of Dr Ambedkar or the most recent developments within the monastic Buddhism of Thailand).

These preliminary remarks are all the more necessary inasmuch as I restrict myself in this chapter to the biblical-Islamic tradition; and there, in terms of the phenomenology and theology of religions, one is hardly certain whether the Islamic attitude to faith can be integrated into the biblical mode of belief, or the biblical tradition belongs to overall Islamic tradition.

Even these remarks on the problems arising in the area of the theory of religions show the degree of caution with which the following disquisition is to be received. All I can do is to open up a number of avenues of thought, stages in my own examination of the subject – an examination which is still far from complete because it is still wholly enmeshed in the experiential process.

### *1. The universal reference of the religions in question*

Theologians of the three great prophetic religions under consideration here for the most part focus the requirement of mundane reference on the message of peace. Peace, however, even in a non-religious connection, has quasi-religious connotations. That is apparent even in political, sociological or psychological and psychiatric acceptations of this key term. These rhetorical repetitions and this verbal consensus about the extraordinary, numinous value of peace often make it seem that the tactical orientation of world responsibility is already implicit in the notion.

That does not prevent the emphases of peace research from being placed elsewhere. The religions (both religious sciences and theologies) are hardly accepted as partners in dialogue in peace studies or looked on as scientific disciplines.[2] The reasons given for this are that in history the religions either have an effect that is actually restrictive of peace (when the spectre of the Christian crusades and of the Holy War of the Old Testament and the Muslim past is invoked), or that they have not spoken out decisively whenever situations of political or economic repression and injustice have arisen. It is said that the religions have contributed almost nothing to the removal of social alienation and aggression.

Neither the anti-racism campaign of the World Council of Churches, nor the liberation theologians of Latin America, nor attempts of recent years at theological interpretations of Maoism in practice would seem to have done anything to change the social situation in South Africa, South America or China. Rather it seems that these efforts lag behind transformed political and economic conditions. And to date the World Conference of Religions for Peace has been able to do nothing to counter this impression. This is all the more true inasmuch as the disparate situation of Christians and non-Christians or the incongruity between the members of missionary revealed religions and representatives of non-proselytizing mystical religions have an inhibiting effect at these conferences.

Organizations concerned with the promotion of peace and developmental strategies on the part of individual religious groups have as little effect here as isolated non-violent demonstrations. The synagogues, churches and mosques, as a whole, remain concerned with appeals for charitable endeavour which does not require any attack upon the manifest results of the circumstances of domination, but confrontation with the latent causes of violence. Here, however, it often seems that the hierarchies are similarly guilty as latent sources of domination.

How is it still possible to speak of the responsibility toward the world of the religions in the face of such radical critiques of their advertised promotion of the cause of peace?

## *2. Theoretical grounding of responsibility to the world*

The teachings of the individual religions on responsibility to the world are quite clear and binding. They proclaim the requirement of service to the world, but there is a widespread lack of practical means of performing such service. Moreover orthodoxy and even theologically grounded tolerance – the tolerance of people who live with a claim to absolute truth – are, as Paul Levy[3] has shown, extremely dangerous for the world and for its peaceful equilibrium.

But the protest of the prophets – and here to be sure we perceive the strength of the revealed religions which is so neglected by peace studies – is constantly raised against truth systems with their attachment to system and for the most part hierarchical forms of administration.

### (i) Prophetic protest in the Bible and in the Koran

Since Max Weber and Joachim Wach[4] we have been aware of the typology afforded by the sociology of religion of the different forms of authority within religious communities. In them the 'charismatic leader' plays a significant part in the present regard. In a society rendered uncertain through social anomie, he undertakes to interpret symptoms of crisis and proffers solutions. His new nomos calls the previous social order in question at major points and offers a counter-model.[5]

(a) *Charismatic leader*. We might select Elijah or Moses from the past of Israel as mystical politicians of this kind. Even Muḥammad's flight from Mecca to Medina, the Hijra of 622, may be cited in the same connection, as a socio-critical desire for release from the existing system, as a protest against tribal discriminations and tribal judgments. Similarly, though in quite different social and religio-political circumstances, the rejection of John the Baptist and Jesus of Nazareth by civil and religious elites has something to do with their critical distance from the religious system and cultic conventions.[6]

These figures became charismatic leaders (in the Weberian sense) as soon as, without recompense, without any priestly office or function, and without any corresponding ritualized rites of institution, they practised and preached a message of liberation which in their environment found a special response among the 'poor'.

(b) *Against the local deities.* Here the world relevance of the biblical and Islamic revealed religions has a negative, critical content. Neither Yahweh nor Allah is a local deity. They are not, like, for instance, the Canaanite Baal-deities, associated with a specific locality where they are ministered to by a priestly caste. The God who reveals himself cannot be enclosed in religiously determined existential arrangements. The omnipotence and unapproachability of Allah does not allow of self-installation. A permanent crossing of boundaries is necessary in these prophetic traditions – insofar as the charisma is not reinstitutionalized –: a lasting exit from religious and ecclesiastical academies, hierarchical rôles and pious behavioural models with their spiritual and denominational demarcations.[7] The believer is rather a person who 'surrenders himself' to God in the changing conditions of life; he is a 'Muslim'.[8] The believing individual is always on the way from prophetic promise to the longed for fulfilment. Therefore he cannot entrust himself to any local Baal and cannot worship idols.

This kind of disenchantment[9] is discernible at key points in biblical tradition. It is directly related to the total transcendentalization of God. This theme of disenchantment in the prophets is also responsible for the tendency among revolutionaries repeatedly to invoke biblical tradition in order to justify their rejection of conservative religious attempts to legitimate the status quo.

(c) *For the God of Exodus.* Not only the hierarchical church institution conceived sub specie aeternatis but the rôles represented by those institutions have to be relativized. Quite generally, it is possible to say that religions occur in history as a form not only of world-supportive but of world-unsettling power. That is apparent, for instance, in very close relation to the Exodus event in which God revealed Himself as the unassignable and incalculable God of history.[10] 'I am who I shall be', says Yahweh – the living God who ever and again is manifest in migration and in transition as the unmanipulable God.

(ii) Doing the truth

The universal responsibility of the revealed religions appears in close association with this prophetic cry of protest and with this social event of Exodus, even in the content of the cry, which may perhaps be summarized as 'Do what is true'. Orthodox practice is the ultimate criterion of faithful existence, and not orthodoxy or the assumption of the prevailing model of legitimation.

(a) *The knowledge of God as righteousness in practice*

The religion of the Bible unmistakably stresses the close connexion between God and one's neighbour, and, most important of all, between God and those who suffer and are in need or are the impotent victims of social circumstances: 'You shall not oppress a hired servant who is poor and needy, whether he is one of your brethren or one of the sojourners who is in your land within your town; you shall give him his hire on the day he earns it... lest he cry against you to the Lord, and it be sin in you' (Deut. 14–5).

This connection goes so far that to 'know God' and 'love God' means ensuring that the poor and humiliated are treated righteously.[11] Hence Jeremiah leaves us in no doubt about the way in which Yahweh is to be known: 'Woe to him who builds his house by unrighteousness, and his upper rooms by injustice; who makes his neighbour serve him for nothing, and does not give his wages... Do you think you are a king because you are complete in cedar? Did not your father eat and drink and do justice and righteousness? Then it was well with him. He judged the cause of the poor and needy; then it was well. Is not this to know me? says the Lord' (Jer. 22 : 13–5f).

The testimonies about Jesus are in the same prophetic cast.[12] Jesus is emphatic in the Sermon on the Mount: "Not every one who says to me, 'Lord, Lord', shall enter the kingdom of heaven, but he who does the will of my father who is in heaven. On that day many will say to me, 'Lord, Lord, did we not prophecy in your name, and cast out demons in your name, and do many mighty works in your name?' And then will I declare to them,

'I never knew you; depart from me, you evildoers' "(Mt. 7 : 21–3).

This also indicates that it is not restrictions determined by the sociology of religion or denomination and ecclesiastical boundaries which offer guarantees for the proximity of salvation, but only one's inner attitude.[13] It is not external physical initiation and the rite of circumcision which are decisive characteristics, but the 'inner circumcision'.

(b) *'Circumcized hearts' and 'Muslim'*

This prophetic requirement is well known in biblical tradition. Modern interpretations of the Koran[14] (and one has to decide whether this is out of opportunism in regard to European Christians) try to understand the term 'Islam' and 'Muslim' in a universal sense, duly relativizing religious-historical limits and religious-statistical data. Hence Sayyid Abū-l-Alā Maudoodī wrote: 'In a precise sense Islam is a qualitative term. Whoever possesses this quality, no matter what his race or community, country or nation may be, is a Muslim. As the Koran, the Holy Book of Muslims, says, in all nations and in all ages there have been good and upright people who possessed these characteristics; they were all and are Muslims'.[15]

(c) *Love as an ethical principle*

For this reason any monopolistic position on the part of a religion is rejected. The criterion is the 'uncircumcized heart' and 'active surrender to God' (Islam). In this way love is elevated from an ethnocentric or tribalistic restriction. It is neither individual eros or interpersonal sympathy (philia) but a fundamental ethical principle (agape),[16] as is apparent in the value system of New Testament Christianity: 'You have heard that it was said, "You shall love your neighbour and hate your enemy". But I say to you, love your enemies and pray for those who persecute you, so that you may be sons of your Father who is in heaven; for he makes his sun rise on the evil and on the good, and sends rain on the just and on the unjust. For is you love those who love you, what reward have you? Do not even the tax collectors do the same? And if you salute only your brethren, what more are you doing than others? Do not even the Gentiles do the same? You, therefore, must be perfect, as your heavenly Father is perfect' (Mt. 5 : 43–8).

Responsibility for the world, therefore is real responsibility for the world, for the particular environment in which we cannot choose the people we are to love. Love is existing in solidarity with and empathizing with every suffering human being. Doing what is true, practising righteousness, taking responsibility out of love, demand the readiness to confront human suffering in this world. Concern[17] and sensitivity[18] are appropriate to this kind of faithful behaviour which has to be not a private affair but social and supranational. Love is an ethical requirement which goes beyond socio-racial prejudices and social class; it is not a feeling but a decision of the will which has to be translated into political and legal practice. Religious responsibility for the world is then confronted with situations of political power and force.[19]

(iii) The dialectic of friends and strangers
As I have already indicated, the ways of behaving required by love demand the abolition of prejudices based on ethnocentric or racist considerations, so that one can identify globally and in an appropriately human manner with the suffering. Therefore the world responsibility of the revealed religions (but the mystical religions are implicated here too) implied a cancellation of national, denominational and dogmatic egotism. Then cooperation becomes possible with the possible elements of change outside the Church and outside parliament (for instance, in trade unions and in schools). This cooperation can strengthen and help to liberate the suffering[21] if it takes the form of perceiving and representing their interests (those that is, of the underprivileged, oppressed and declaredly alien).[20]

The biblical justification of this social, political and even cultic emancipation of oppressed 'strangers' is located in Deuteronomy in the memory of the collective experience of Israel in foreign lands, in the past of the people of Israel in the work camps of Egypt, and in the Exodus event. During this period of deportation the Israelites experienced what it meant to be a foreigner: 'You shall not pervert the justice due to the sojourner or to the fatherless, or take a widow's garment in pledge; but you shall remember that you were a slave in Egypt... therefore I command you to do this' (Deut. 24 : 17–8).

Nevertheless this experience of foreigness in the past is not the exclusive reason for solidarity with the stranger. Much more, past existence as socio-cultural aliens in Egypt is extended theologically to the present understanding of existence. Before God, indeed, man is always a stranger. This is the basic attitude which David recalls for the people in his farewell prayer: 'For we are strangers before thee, and sojourners, as all our fathers were; our days on earth are like a shadow, and there is no abiding' (1 Chron. 29 : 15).

Consequently the socio-ethical motivation for this positive attitude to the foreigner and the stranger is mystical: the same certainty for Israelites and non-Israelites that they are 'alien', not at home, not secure with God.[22] This general denominator offers the same presuppositions for living. Accordingly geographical foreignness, social distinction, racial difference and national consciousness are relativized in principle. Internationalism is a basic requirement of the religious understanding of the world in the monotheistic religious tradition as well.[23]

### *3. Ways to universal responsibility of the religions*

But how can this mysticism become a methodology and a strategy? What kind of practical theory can we propose? What didactic means are appropriate? It is a matter of finding a technique of conversion, structures of reconciliation and means of dialogue which will allow us to promote responsibility for the world in searching for peace and in hope of fulfilment of the great promises. It is possible to study only individual cases in this transition from homily to pastoral, from worship to political practice. What we need is a casuistics. What do the revealed religions have to say and to offer in this regard?

(i) De-alienation

In descent from the above-mentioned demystification of the numinous and of ideological taboos which derives above all from the prophetic stance of protest, there would seem to be a possibility for the religions to take action in a way that would not support but undermine domination. Religion is not necessarily the opium of the people.[24] On the contrary, the charismatic leader can overthrow existing secular structures and the procedures that legitimate and support them. He can promote a universal religious freedom wherever the religions are as it were sequestrated by the state.

(a) *The struggle against the powers*

The theme of the powers and rulers of this world in the New Testament is a very promising approach in this regard.[25] The various labels and titles – some personal, some impersonal – used to describe this realm of the powers that dominate this world indicate a diffuse phenomenon which sorely besets all people.[26] To be sure, these terms are not categorized or systematized in the form of an angelology or demonology, yet the reality of these anonymous, intangible and yet omnipresent powers is clearly indicated. The believer is called on to oppose these powers, which are manifested in the physical (illnesses and possession, for example), mental (according to Paul, for example, fear of the law or of the ritual prescriptions of the mythical religions), or social realms (according to the Book or Revelation, for instance). All creatures of power have to be deprived of their power. They may not remain rulers of this world. The actual responsibility for the world of the religions has to confront these powers: 'For we are not contending against flesh and blood, but against the principalities, against the powers, against the world rulers of this present darkness, against the spiritual hosts of wickedness in the heavenly places' (Eph. 6 : 12).

The believer has to be direct and far from naive in his dealings with these deadly powers, which are 'in the atmosphere', which he 'breathes in', and has to confront the suffering which they provoke. The religions have to do everything they can to provide space, and in so doing a beacon within their communities, which is not ruled by these anonymous powers – nowadays Galtung's term is appropriate: by these 'structures of domination'. The overthrow of these forms of repression within one's own 'church' is precisely the sign of its authenticity and credibility, if the universal responsibility of the religions is in question. Here we have a criterion for deciding that struggle and 'holy war' are part not only of the everyday reality of the religions but of their contribution to 'mobilization for peace'.

(b) *Distance of rôles*

In this struggle to relativize and neutralize all powers within and outside the Church, the loss and surrender of prestige in ecclesiastical rôles becomes a major strategy. Above all the mystical tendencies within the revealed religions too (in addition to their prophetic protest) have developed a useful form of tactics. The mystic experiences every temporal reality within this world as anticipatory. In this way his mystico-meditative experience of himself and of the social system enables him to obtain distance from himself and from the social system – the social consequence of kenosis. Mystical experiences of this kind make the world relative, as well as its organizations, institutions, prescriptions, classifications, behavioural norms and symbols of prestige.[27] The world is experience in its aspect of finiteness. It is not that which is ultimately binding.[28]

Since religions as socio-cultural systems are only something penultimate, just like the world, the individual with mystical experience of transcendence can change his immanent, public behaviour: (i) in regard to the taboo ceremonies and rites in the religious or civil field (he continues to take part in them, but treats them in an 'as-if' sense); (ii) by resisting the idols of the fixed nomoi; (iii) by demystifying the state and religion, and denying the binding nature of their attempts at legitimation.

As we shall see, this inner experience of faith affords not only negative protest but the positive spontaneity and freedom to discover new behavioural patterns or to abandon internalized models. The rigidity and formalism of the pressure exerted by institutional norms are offset in this way. Hence the religions contribute to de-alienation:[29] individual interests are reflected in this kind of conversion, and prejudices are removed.

(b) *Dialogue and conflict*

These biblical and Islamic themes of struggle against the powers, and this orientation of meditation towards education for peace, also afford a certain tendency to conflict.[30] This, however, does not prevent progress towards conciliation but desentimentalizes it. Pain and rigour are not removed from this process of conversion (in this respect we have only to remember the religious martyrs, who were often killed by their own co-religionists), but they are deflected from the life-and-death struggle of the world's striving for profit and power in order to engage in the war of liberation against striving for profit and power in the personal and public, religious and non-religious fields. This struggle 'to the last' – right up to the sacrifice of one's own life – is intended to destroy the fight for power in one's self and in others. Therefore this struggle for the 'discernment of spirits' neither destroys nor absorbs the individual, but is concerned for and delivers him or her:

*the* individual: that is, all individuals engaged in the struggle, even the oppressors.

In this way the conflict becomes a form of life, a religious form of life as well, a religious category.[31] But it is no longer a matter of getting rid of the opponent, but of developing appropriate mechanisms of compromise and conversion which try to remove all striving towards even dogmatic postulations of absolutes. That is difficult to achieve precisely in the case of the prophetic religions. Therefore it is all the more important consciously to pursue and verbalize all conflitcs. Then 'conflict' no longer has the status of existential aggression, but that of 'incompatibility between the goals or conceived values of the agents of a social system' (Galtung), of a specific religion.

If we speak universally in such a context of the responsibility for the world of religions, certainly an initial concern is to see, acknowledge and live with these diverse goals in the social, theological and psychological sectors. This immense intellectual and emotional demand on the parties to conflict and on the religions rent by disputes is hardly even desired let alone acted upon. Hence the attempts at dialogue and meetings for dialogue proceed so unrealistically for the most part – and therefore those researching into conflict and peace can count on so poor a contribution from the religions. Then religions are much more liable to contribute to the suppression than the vitalization of conflict or, as often happens in 'ecumenical' conferences[32], merely assist a purely ceremonial and liturgical resolution of conflicts.[33]

(iii) Contemplation and commitment

Both Mahatma Gandhi and, for example, the Latin American theologians of liberation have considered these connections between the prophetico-mystical orientation of religions and politico-social action. This synthesis between the 'militant' and the 'contemplative' is all the more pressing since the experience of Christians in encounter with the person of Jesus leads to contemplative experience of the presence of Christ in one's brothers or sisters. In the well-known Matthew pericope 25 : 31ff we find the relevant prototype: '... for I was hungry and you gave me food... as you did it to one of the least of these my brethren, you did it to me'. Here encounter with the suffering and needy in the world and the consequent responsibility of service constitute awareness of Christ. Hence they are both contemplative experience and personal encounter with the Lord.

(a) *Every human being is a temple of God*

This kind of inward perception is only attainable by means of the meditative conviction that every human being represents God and is a 'temple of the Holy Spirit'. This divine presence even in the person whom we would designate as a social or national enemy is a prerequisite for the assumption of responsibility for the world (which says nothing about the choice between violent or peaceful means). Then love becomes a political mode, since it does not allow sociological reality to dictate the boundaries of trustful openness and receptivity. Hence the believer is forced to abandon himself and the system – to convert. Charismatic perception makes him or her a critical participant in the officialized and institutionalized charisma which lives on in the particular community of faith.

Spiritual homelessness becomes a way of life in this tension between charisma and institution within resposibility for the 'world' (not only of the 'cosmos' but of the oikumene – the 'whole inhabited world'). In this kind of attitude of spiritual alienation, the mystic and the peace researcher exist somewhere between the establishment and the people,[34] between the hierarchy of privileged power élites and the masses against whom they discriminate. There they attempt to assume responsibility for the world in practice and not rhetorically.

(b) *Homelessness as a political attitude*

Then mystical experience is not merely published and preached in oral discourse but is also expressed socially. The road to 'spiritual homelessness', the expectation of 'Christ outside the walls of the church', transference to the land of spiritual aliens, are call-signs of this prophetico-mystical mode of existence. It is not social repression which dictates alienation and homelessness (say, as a political refugee) but the spiritual motif of the peregrinatio religiosa.[35] This theme of choosing 'alienation for the sake of God' accords with the aforementioned 'dialectic of neighbour and stranger'. This experience that both neighbour and stranger are 'God's temples' avoids any cheap, pseudo-mystical conceptualism. Rather the mystic must mark out in anticipatory hardship the social alienation in political and ecclesiastical structures.[36] Then the mystical approach enters the social structure.

### 4. *'Shalom' as a theo-political model of practical orientation to the world by the revealed religions*

The ways proposed for orientation to the world by the revealed religions (de-alienation, rôle distancing, de-absolutization, spiritual homelessness) certainly still appears too impractical, too mystical and removed from the world. I am, however, convinced that in work for peace the religions can counteract the danger of resignation or the risk of demagogic activism precisely by means of this mystical securing of economic, sociological, and psychoanalytical strategies. The chances of influence on world-historical events, the possibility of examining personal interests, the attempt to remove prejudices, and the de-monopolization[37] of ideologies and theologies are the prerequisites for any assumption of responsibility for *the world*. Otherwise it would be a matter of no more than responsibility for the *particular world,* for one's own specific circumambient universe. A final consideration of the dimensions of shalom will show this more clearly.

(i) The ambiguous nature of the concept of shalom

The 'establishment of shalom' may certainly be proposed as the content of the responsibility for the world of biblical, Christian and Islamic religion. Shalom in this regard (cf. Ps. 85) may be described as peace, joy, freedom, integrity, conciliation, community, harmony, justice, truth, communication. This multidimensional conception of shalom reveals on the one hand its soteriological thrust, and on the other hand its social orientation.

(a) *Shalom as an open concept*

The multidimensional and pluriform nature of the notion of shalom indicates that it is not a firmly determined but an 'open' term. It indicates the simultaneous achievement of a number of salvific instances which are not demonstrable in advance. Hoekendijk, who speaks in this connection of the 'shalomization of life as a whole', says: 'Therefore we can never reduce shalom to a simple formula to be applied in all circumstances which might arise. Shalom must be discovered and formed in actual situations'.[38] Hence we may call shalom a 'theo-political' concept. All characterizations of shalom refer indeed to secular social concerns. What shalom means is 'discovered, assured and attained... in actual co-existence with those for whom shalom is intended'. Shalom is a social event, an event of interhuman relations, a concern of human solidarity. In this sense, however, shalom is also a theological concept: one cannot possess God's salvation without sharing it with those most in need of it.

The call-sign shalom therefore comprises, in this perspective, a combination of salvation history and mundane event. It relates the soteriologico-eschatological elements of the kingdom of God directly to the historico-social reality of human beings. Shalom so unites the kingdom of God and the world that they become inseparable.

(b) *Shalom as a closed concept*

Nowadays a certain, often pietistic use of the word shalom tends to make it a watchword or a myth which traduces the ancient eastern lines of the concept. It is necessary to remember this primarily on literary and textual grounds. It is also important because we are thereby reminded of a danger which arises whenever religions are in question. In their orientation to the world, which I have summarized here as orientation to peace, the religions run the risk of reducing peace to 'their' peace. A short analysis of the notion of shalom will show this more clearly.[39]

The practical and textual contexts of talk of peace in ancient middle-eastern tradition (Egyptian, Sumerian, Mesopotamian) are the rituals of enthronement, descriptions of the origins, and certain 'historical' texts which refer to specific events in the particular national history. What is clearly apparent in these enthronement rituals, recalling the original order of creation and the retelling of historical heroic deed, is the often limited, ethnocentric image of peace. Above all in the political aspect of this peace it is often apparent that 'peace' does not refer to, say, peaceful coexistence with other nations, but to their subjection. The logic operating in these reports is as follows: The 'world-order', however comprehensive it may be portrayed as being, is actually that of the particular state, of the particular group. The 'world' order in Egypt, Mesopotamia or Sumeria, is the order of the Egyptian, Mesopotamian or Sumerian world. Hence part of that order, precisely in regard to peace, is the subjection of the enemy, the 'pacification' of other nations. The enemy, the foreigner, the 'unbeliever' belongs to the side of chaos, to the side of the powers that threaten the cosmos. And again, universal peace is the universal peace of Egypt (MaaT), the universal peace of Mesopotamia, the universal peace of Sumeria. The other nations are considered only negatively, as disturbers of order –only as 'subject peoples' do they have any share in this 'peace'.

On looking back at history – one thinks of certain biblical psalms of commination and of the self-abasement of the nations on the occasion of the 'pilgrimage of the nations' to Mount Sion, or of the aggressive interpretations of 'Holy War' and the 'crusades' in the Islamic and Christian past and present – one sees that Israel, Christianity and Islam to a great extent still share this ethnocentric, 'universalist tendency' with the ancient middle-eastern world-views. This is also shown by the originally restrictive understanding of the commandment, 'Thou shalt not kill'. This commandment forbids before all else, of course, only the pursuit of a vendetta off one's own bat and without reference to the community. Therefore it forbids only the shedding of blood in one's own bedouin group, in one's own nation and clan. The corresponding notion of God is that He is primarily the God of one's own people – whether the Israelite, the white man, or the Arab. Even today our particular religions are still too often henotheistic and not sufficiently monotheistic.

(ii) Peace and human identification

Therefore the thrust of the religions is certainly independent of nationalism in throry and in a mystical sense, but in the everyday world of security and politics it is still often subsumed into state efforts. And yet the religions could not adopt that viewpoint which holds that the world must consist of self-defining nations. On the contrary, the believer should transcend these antagonisms, as I tried to do with the model of the 'circumcized heart' and the 'Muslim'. In contradistinction to identification with a nation or a religion, he or she represents as a loving person a universal form of identification: the liberation of every individual from every thing which stands against his or her self-realization.[40] Nations and religions are abstractions, and immanent to the system – and systems cannot encounter one another. National and denominational interests are meaningless so long as they are not the interests of the humblest but only the interests of a dwindling ecclesialistical or political élite.

The universal call to salvation and human identification one with the other are meaningful only if these perspectives of a caring humanity and the corresponding planning of reconciliatory responsibility for the world are expressed in identification with the oppressed, with the 'sinners' and 'unbelievers'. Only thus can the world-orientated struggle against structural force – what has been termed in a biblical sense the 'powers and rulers' – become meaningful.

(iii) The future of religions as transnational pressure-groups

Strong erosive forces are already at work on the classical nation-state of the type that came into being in Europe a few centuries ago and is now imitated by most of the third-world nations. In so far as the religions represent ethnic and national interests, here too they run the risk of being compelled to change their ideas in the face of economic and political reality. More and more people are inclined to identify with more than one nation. They do this because as a result of 'circulation'[41] they increasingly come into contact with people from other countries: because they are marrred to a man or a woman from another country, go to work abroad, are employed by international organizations, or exist at some point in the industrial network of the multinationals. And surely more and more people tend to identify with more than one religion.

In the sense of a broader ecumenism – or 'communionism', as Archbishop Fernandes of New Delhi said in regard to the World Conference of Religions for Peace[42] – the starting-point of encounter between religions would no longer be dogmatic loyalties and discrepancies, but the common goal of 'religionists' in the world – undertaking responsibility for the realization of human rights, social justice and the end of racism.

Therefore it is a matter of ensuring that the religions no longer allow themselves to be outdone by politics, but in prophetic freedom show their solidarity with people who do not in the manner of proselytizers wish to take over others' world, but try in the world to point in an exemplary fashion to the coming of the kingdom of God. The time for controversial theology between religions has also gone by. We are on the way to a theology of co-operation which shows its sense of responsibility for the world.

# Notes

1 On this question of the extent of the notion and process of revelation (and its significance for the universal religions in the perspective of the theology of religions), see: D.S. Amalorpavadass (Ed.), Research Seminar on Non-Biblical Scriptures (Bangladore, 1975).

2 Cf. in this regard Johan Galtung's investigation of the scientific disciplines engaged in seventy institutions concerned with peace research, and those disciplines considered significant: J. Galtung, 'Friedensforschung', in: E. Krippendorff (Ed.), Friedensforschung (Cologne & Berlin, 1970), pp. 520–4. It is possible at best to include religions and theologies in sociology (77%) and under the themes of anti-Semitism (16%) and ethnocentrism (25%).

3 P. Levy, Une paix pour notre temps (Gembloux, 1975).

4 J. Wash, Religionssoziologie (Tübingen, [4]1951), pp. 375–422; M. Weber, Wirtschaft und Gesellschaft (Cologne & Berlin 1964) pp. 160–87, especially pp. 182 and 187.

5 See in this connection the linguistic and cultural-anthropological investigations of the Jamaa family movement begun by Placide Tempel in the anomic colonial situation of Katanga: J. Fabian, Jamaa: A Charismatic Movement in Katanga (Evanston, 1971), pp. 84, 88–92.

6 Cf. F. Belo, Lecture matérialiste de l'évangile de Marc (Paris, 1974).

7 See on these transitions, P.L. Berger, Zur Dialektik von Religion und Gesellschaft (Tübingen, 1973), pp. 108–21.

8 Sayyid Abū-l-Alā Maudoodī, Weltanschauung und Leben im Islam (Freiburg im Breisgau, 1971), pp. 15, 52, 89, 113, 141.

9 Berger, op. cit., p. 96: 'In biblical tradition, the social order was so relativized by confrontation with the majesty of the transcendent God, that it is actually possible to speak of the end of alienation – in the sense that before the countenance of God institutions were shown to be no more than human products without any inherent sacredness and immortality'.

10 On the Exodus event, see: J.C. Hoekendij, Kirche und Volk in der deutschen Missionswissenschaft (Munich, 1967), pp. 348–9; D. Manecke, Mission als Zeugendienst (Wuppertal, 1972), pp. 136–8 (the God of Exodus and Baal); J. Moltmann, Kirche in der Kraft des Geistes (Munich, 1975), pp. 93–103.

11 G. Gutiérrez, A Theology of Liberation (New York, 1972; London, 1974), pp. 160–77 (conversion to one's neighbour).

12 See Is. 1:10–7; 58:6-11.

13 On this dividing-line, which is not sociologically discernible but runs somewhere between the indifferent and those concerned for others, between the haves and the have-nots, see: R. Friedli, Fremdheit als Heimat (Freiburg, 1974), pp. 147, 195–200.

14 Maudoodi, op. cit., p. 141: 'In previous chapters I said that all prophets who have appeared from time to time have proclaimed Islam. This is a very important fact. The prophets proclaimed Islam, that means belief in God with all his characteristics, belief in the Last Judgment, belief in divine messengers and the revealed books, and consequently they summoned people to lead a life of obedience and surrender to their Lord. That is what is understood as Din, and on that the teachings of all prophets were grounded'. See also pp. 15 and 113.

15 Ibid., p. 15.

16 Cf. in this respect, A. Nygren, Agape and Eros (London, 1932-9, 2 vols.).

17 On 'being concerned', see H.-E. Bahr (Ed.), Politisierung des Alltags: gesellschaftliche Bedingungen des Friedens (Darmstadt & Neuwied, 1972), pp. 23–4 (forms of concern).

18 See H.J. Margull, 'Verwundbarkeit. Bemerkungen zum Dialog', in: Evangelische Theologie 34–5 (1974), pp. 410–20.

[19] J. Galtung, Strukturelle Gewalt (Reinbek bei Hamburg, 1975), p. 47.

[20] See above all the proclamation of Jesus which has become a central citation in Black and Latin American liberation theology: 'The Spirit of the Lord is upon me, because he has anointed me to preach good news to the poor. He has sent me to proclaim release to the captives and recovering of sight to the blind, to set at liberty those who are oppressed, to proclaim the acceptable year of the Lord' – Lk. 4 : 19–9; comparison of this quotation with Is. 61 : 1–2 shows that an interiorized, individually spiritual interpretation of this text would be too one-sided.

[21] See in this regard: C. Wulf (Ed.), Kritische Friedenserziehung (Frankfurt am Main, 1973), pp. 126–7.

[22] See in this regard also Ps. 119 : 19; 39 : 13; Jer. 35 : 7; on the whole topic: Friedli, Fremdheit als Heimat, op. cit., pp. 137–49.

[23] This international orientation is emphasized in' R. Agneau & D. Pryen, Après la mission. Christianisme et espoirs de libération (Paris, 1975), pp. 223–49, esp. 247–8 (with reference to F. Belo, op. cit.).

[24] See Moltmann, op. cit., p. 93, for the view that religion is faced with more than the danger of a religion of consolation.

[25] On the following see: H. Schlier, Mächte und Gewalten im Neuen Testament (Freiburg im Breisgau, 1959).

[26] In the basic faith of Islam in the first Kalima 'lā ilāha illā-llāh', this constellation of powers in the world is also testified to – and relativized: 'There is no god apart from God'. See Maudoodi's commentary, op. cit., pp. 90–106, esp. 99: 'That is the meaning of 'lā ilāha' – there is *absolutely* no god; no human creature and no material thing, no material object possesses divine powers and authority which are worth worship, subjection and obedience and would justify them'. Schlier's exposition on 'powers and rulers' draws the same socio-critical consequences from monotheism.

[27] These 'highly-revolutionary sociological implications of monotheism' (Prof. Askari) can be traced biographically in the life of the Sufi martyr El-Hallaj. See L. Massignon, Al-Hallaj. Martyr mystique de l'Islam (Paris, 1922).

[28] On this power of mysticism to cancel alienation and to effect social rôles only in an as–if attitude, see Berger, op. cit., pp. 94–8.

[29] Ibid., pp. 84, 89, 93, 121 (disenchantment, de-alienation).

[30] P. Hünermann & H.-D. Fischer (Eds.), Gott im Aufbruch (Freiburg im Breisgau, 1974), pp. 140–5.

[31] On this topic of struggle as a theological category see R.L. Whitehead, 'Love and Animosity in the Ethics of Mao', in: Lutheran World Federation/Pro Mundi Vita, Theological Implications of the New China (Geneva & Brussels, 1974), pp. 79–81 (a theology of struggle): N.P. Moritzen & W.H. Willeke (Eds.), China – Herausforderung an die Kirchen (Erlangen, 1974, 78–9) (theme of struggle in the New Testament).

[32] On the notion of ecumenism raised here: R. Friedli, 'Dialoge mit buddhistischen Menschen aus Thailand', in' Zeitschrift für Missionswissenschaft und Religionswissenschaft (Münster), 59/2 (1975), pp. 81–94, esp. 82–5.

[33] Galtung, Strukturelle Gewalt, op. cit., p. 129.

[34] Ibid., pp. 51, 58.

[35] See R. Friedli, 'Kulturelle Zirkulation als Impuls einer Theologie der Religionen', in: Freiburger Zeitschrift für Philosophie und Theologie (Freiburg im Breisgau), 21/1 (1974), pp. 236–59.

[36] Berger, op. cit., pp. 144–5 (demonopolization and crisis of faith as a socio-structural problem).

[37] On the term shalom, see H.H. Schmid, Frieden ohne Illusionen (Zürich, 1971); C. Westermann, 'Der Frieden (shalom) im Alten Testament', in: Studien zur Friedensforschung, 1 (Stuttgart, 1969), pp. 144–77.

[38] J.C. Hoekendijk, op. cit., p. 347; Manecke, op. cit., pp. 141–4.

[39] Schmid, op. cit., pp. 9–20.

[40] Galtung, Strukturelle Gewalt, op. cit., p. 51.

[41] On the phenomenon of 'circulation', see R. Friedli, Fremdheit als Heimat, op. cit., pp. 31–77.

[42] A. Fernandes, Religion and a New World Order (New Delhi, 1976).

## Contributors

*Heinrich Gross* is Professor of Old Testament Exegesis at the University of Regensburg, Federal Republic of Germany.

*Albert H. Friedlander* is a Rabbi and Principal of Leo Baeck College, London.

*Abdoldjavad Falaturi* is Professor of Islamology and Philosophy at the University of Cologne, Federal Republic of Germany.

*Jakob J. Petuchowski* is Research Professor in Jewish Theology and Liturgy at Hebrew Union College/Jewish Institute of Religion, Cincinnati, Ohio, USA.

*Michael Brocke* is a Lecturer in Judaic Studies in the Catholic theological faculty of the University of Regensburg, Federal Republic of Germany.

*Erwin Gräf* was until his death in February 1976 Professor of Islamology at the University of Cologne, Federal Republic of Germany.

*Michael Winter* is an Islamicist at the University of Tel Aviv, Israel.

*Hasan Askari* is Professor of the Sociology of Religion in the Department of Sociology, Aligarh Muslim University, Aligarh, India.

*Wilhelm Dantine* is Professor of Systematic Theology in the Protestant Theological Faculty of the University of Vienna, Austria.

*Engelbert Mveng*, SJ, is a Professor at the University of Yaoundé, Cameroon.

*Richard Friedli* is Professor of Missiology at the University of Fribourg, Switzerland.